John Washington's Civil War

John Washington's
CIVIL WAR

A Slave Narrative

Edited, with an Introduction and Notes, by
CRANDALL SHIFFLETT

Louisiana State University Press
Baton Rouge

Published by Louisiana State University Press
New material copyright © 2008 by Louisiana State University Press
All rights reserved
Manufactured in the United States of America
First printing

Designer: Michelle A. Neustrom
Typeface: ITC Cushing BT
Printer and binder: Thomson-Shore, Inc.

Library of Congress Cataloging-in-Publication Data

Washington, John, 1838–1918.
  John Washington's Civil War : a slave narrative / edited, with an introduction and
notes, by Crandall Shifflett.
    p. cm.
  Includes bibliographical references and index.
  ISBN 978-0-8071-3301-9 (cloth : alk. paper) — ISBN 978-0-8071-3302-6 (pbk. : alk.
paper) 1. Washington, John, 1838–1918. 2. Fugitive slaves—United States—Biography. 3. Slaves—Virginia—Fredericksburg—Biography. 4. Fredericksburg (Va.)—
History—19th century. 5. Virginia—History—Civil War, 1861–1865—Personal narratives. 6. United States—History—Civil War, 1861–1865—Personal narratives.
7. United States—History—Civil War, 1861–1865—African Americans. 8. African Americans—Biography. 9. Slave narratives—United States. 10. Fredericksburg
(Va.)—Biography. I. Shifflett, Crandall A. II. Title.
  E450.W325A3 2008
  973.7'115092—dc22
  [B]

                                                            2007025213

For Myrtle and the late Maurice Bredeson,
a warm hearth in a cold land

CONTENTS

ILLUSTRATIONS

PREFACE

On 18 April 1862, John Washington, a 24-year-old slave hired out by his owner, Catherine Taliaferro, to James Mazeen, was serving breakfast at the eating saloon in the Shakespeare Hotel in Fredericksburg, Virginia. The breakfast crowd on that Good Friday was restless because "a rumor had been circulated among them that the Yankees Was advancing." Suddenly, several cannon reports sounded, and "in an instant all Was Wild confusion as a cavalry Man dashed into the Dining Room and Said 'The Yankees is in Falmouth.'" A scramble for the door ensued. Mazeen came running up to Washington "and thrust a roll of Bank notes in my hand and hurriedly told me to pay off all the Servants, and Shut up the house and take charge of every thing." Mazeen warned Washington that if the Yankees caught him they would kill him. "In less time than it takes me to Write these lines, every White Man was out of the house. Every Man servant was out on the house top looking over the River at the Yankees [whose] glistening bayonets could easily be Seen." Washington continues this remarkable account with a description of retreating Rebels burning the town's bridges and scenes of stores being closed while white residents scurried about trying to hide.

In the early 1990s, while working in the collections of the Library of Congress on Civil War Fredericksburg, I first came across an index entry on John Washington, "Memorys of the Past." As I recall, it was described as a slave narrative. The description immediately aroused my interest and excitement. About 120 autobiographical slave narratives were published before the Civil War and another 100 afterwards. Some of the most well known narratives include those of Frederick Douglass, Harriet Jacobs, and most recently a fictionalized account of the life of Hannah Crafts. Newly discovered first-hand accounts of slavery are very rare. As I looked at the microfilm, I saw that here was an account of a man's life from his birth as a slave in 1838 until 1872, when the narrative was written—years that spanned the most momentous period in the history of our nation, and in his own handwriting.

John Washington's "Memorys of the Past" does not reflect the intellectual depth or eloquence of a Frederick Douglass. Until the Civil War, Washington never lived outside a radius of seventy-five miles in Virginia. While Douglass circulated among public figures in the press and abolitionist societies, where he honed his skills in writing and public speaking, Washington's contacts were limited mostly to small slaveholders, white farmers, small-town merchants, a few white preachers and schoolteachers, and the free blacks and slaves he met while being hired out in Richmond and Fredericksburg to a tobacco manufacturer and hotel-saloon keepers. Douglass's writings and speeches demonstrate his broad ambitions to speak for African Americans generally, and Douglass's narratives reflect his public performances. He refined his words before hundreds of audiences, and in our time, Douglass's utterances have been used to articulate civil rights struggles and his writings have become classics of American literature. Washington, on the other hand, confined his observations to the local society he had known, and his recollections remained private during his lifetime. Washington's writings are unpracticed, but he is by no means inarticulate. Although confined to a small corner of eastern Virginia, Washington's recollections give us a glimpse of a war that on Good Friday 1862 was not officially about slavery. To a young slave, however, those cannon blasts were ushering in the end of the local institution of slavery, and Washington's observations can do what no practiced eloquence can achieve: bear eyewitness from the slave's point of view.

Despite their differences, in interesting ways Washington's experiences parallel those of Douglass. Each was the son of a slave woman and an unknown white man, at least unknown so far as can be discerned from their writings. They grew up in adjacent areas of the Chesapeake. Both experienced painful separations from their mothers and other family members at an early age. Humiliating and cruel beatings, which Douglass received and Washington only witnessed, in both cases generated a most intense hatred of the institution of slavery that drove their resolve to escape. Gaining literacy in the South where whites were prohibited from teaching slaves to read and write gave both men the chance to seize freedom when the opportunity came. Both writers were young when they escaped slavery and when they wrote their recollections of slave life. Douglass escaped bondage at age twenty; Washington was twenty-four when the Union army arrived. Douglass published his first life story *(Narrative of the Life of Frederick Douglass)* at the age of twenty-seven and his second *(My Bondage and My Freedom)* at age thirty-seven, while Washington penned his recollections at thirty-four. (Douglass went on to publish more autobiographies in 1882, 1892, and 1893.)

Since discovering Washington's narrative, I have presented papers on it at annual meetings of the Organization of American Historians in Anaheim, California, in 1993 and the Southern Historical Association in Birmingham, Alabama, in 1998; had press editors read it; and used it in my classes on southern history. It never fails to bring expressions of astonishment. Why? Because here is a narrative that effectively communicates in the most salient ways an understanding of what it meant to be a slave and live through the Civil War. After all, slavery through the eyes of slaves is what makes the Works Progress Administration collection of slave narratives of the 1930s such a treasure. Those depression-era recollections caused historians to rethink, revise, and ultimately rewrite the history of antebellum slavery. Yet for all their value and merit—and it is substantial—those narratives cannot compare to recollections like "Memorys." Few are as compelling as a work composed within seven years of the end of slavery. Between 1865 and the recording of the WPA narratives, nearly seventy years intervened. Former slaves had lived a lot of history, and memories had dimmed, suffered distortion, or taken on new meaning as they were refracted through the prism of nearly three quarters of a century in time and experience.

On the other hand, the urgency, immediacy, and contingency of history in time and space come alive in "Memorys" because of the direct contact between biography, place, and time, allowing present generations to get inside the head of a slave and understand the experience of slavery and war intimately. I am happy to be able to share this narrative with many types of readers: classroom teachers, professional historians, and general readers who want to learn more about this period of history from the vantage point of a slave who lived during these days of drums and years of bugles, sounding the end of a way of life for some and the notes of freedom for others.

As is true with nearly all slave narratives, whether those of Washington, Douglass, Harriet Jacobs, or Hannah Crafts, individual reactions, treatment, or conditions of labor may differ, but the slave angle of vision sometimes makes familiar historical questions appear simplistic, irrelevant, or condescending. Through the eyes of John Washington, we chance to see a different world than most whites imagined. "Memorys" gives us the opportunity to direct questions to the slaves themselves. When extra rations were given at Christmastime, for example, did the slaves believe it was an act of kindness or something else? Did forcing slaves to attend church make them more tractable and religious? What did Washington think when whites told him the Yankees would cut off his hands if they captured him? How did slaves and masters interpret occasions such as fairs, corn shuckings, hog killings, and other celebratory events?

John Washington and many other slaves and free blacks personified the ideals of autonomy, liberty, and equity. A substantial minority of white Fredericksburgers, most notably flour miller Joseph Ficklin and antislavery figure Mary Minor Blackford, cherished liberty and fair treatment for blacks, despite reservations about black equality. Washington's masters, owners, and their supporters—as seen in owner Catherine Taliaferro (a.k.a. Mrs. Nathaniel Ware), diarist Betty Maury, preacher Horace Lacy, geographer Matthew Fontaine Maury, and countless other loyal Confederate sympathizers—personified a different set of ideals: authority, control, and patriarchy. Recognizing nuances of opinion and the pitfalls of drawing lines too sharply, we may still see that two mental worlds arose out of the different circumstances of birth, status, time, and geography.

As people and history intersect during periods of crisis, cherished values and ideals seem to rush to the surface. That is what makes wars, revolutions, and other large-scale events valuable to historians and students of the past. As the Civil War approached, for example, the Washington world view distilled its immediate hopes and aspirations into heady dreams of freedom. Freedom of choice, freedom of movement, freedom to keep what was earned—these long-denied natural rights, once unthinkable, now suddenly seemed within reach. Few slaves could anticipate how elusive they would become during the emancipation period and even more so with the onset of Jim Crow segregation. The Taliaferro-Ware world view placed its hopes upon autonomy and control mediated through the patriarchy, with "family" including everyone in the master's household hierarchy from the master down to wife, children, and slaves.

For most planters, the war was about preserving a way of life; this was their understanding of freedom. The clash of these two mental worlds recurs over and over again in "Memorys of the Past."

Librarians, colleagues, students, friends, press readers, a foundation, and family members have supported me during the research and writing of this book. My work on Civil War Fredericksburg began in 1992, and I presented several papers on my research at professional conventions. A National Endowment for the Humanities Fellowship for College Teachers and Independent Scholars in 1995 gave me the gift of six months of "free time" to devote to research. Virginia Tech and its History Department allowed me the leave time to pursue the research. Librarians and archivists at the National Archives, the James Madison Room of the Library of Congress, the University of Virginia's Alderman Library and its Geospatial and Statistical Center, the Virginia Military Institute Archives, and the Central Rappahannock Regional Library in Fredericksburg were most accommodating to all my requests. A special thanks to Robert K. Krick, Chief Historian, National Parks Service, who made his library available to me early in the research. Progress on this work slowed in 1997 when I took on a project called "Virtual Jamestown," and again in 2005–2006 when I answered a call to be interim director of the Center for Digital History at the University of Virginia. While at the Center, Madelyn Wessel was—and has been since—the source of sound advice and wise counsel. The staff of Louisiana State University Press has been a delight to work with. I thank Rand Dotson, acquisitions editor, for his encouragement to complete this project, and Catherine Kadair, senior editor, for her clever suggestions on narrative presentation and attentive copy editing. Mary Lee Eggart drew the beautiful maps. An anonymous and well-informed press reader greatly improved the final manuscript. I want to thank my friend Joseph Miller at the University of Virginia, who sets a high standard with his own teaching, scholarship, and contributions to the profession, for pointing me to Calvin Schermerhorn, his Ph.D. student and a promising historian. In the final stages of the manuscript, Calvin provided expert assistance from his own knowledge and work in southern history. My special thanks to Barbara, my wife, a model teacher of American history, and a wonderful lifelong companion. It is to her parents that this book is dedicated.

As this book reached the final stages of production, David W. Blight published *A Slave No More: Two Men Who Escaped to Freedom, Including Their Own Narratives of Emancipation* (Harcourt, Inc., 2007). His book is built around John Washington's "Memorys" and another slave narrative by Wallace Turnage. I had been working on the Washington recollection for nearly a decade and a half, interrupted by my ever-demanding and successful Virtual Jamestown project, when I read an article in the *New York Times* on 14 June 2004 about Blight's "newly discovered narratives." From Blight's book I learned the entire story of how he got involved in this project. He did not "discover" the Washington recollection, as the *New York Times* said in its 2004 article and as William Grimes said again in his review for the *Times* on 5 December 2007. In his prologue, Blight says this book "found me in a rather unusual way." He had been approached by a literary agent working on behalf of Julian Houston, a retired Boston judge who had inherited Washington's writings and papers from his mother, who had in turn gotten them as a best friend of Washington's granddaughter (Evelyn Easterly). Houston had placed the Washington narrative on deposit at the Massachusetts Historical Society "for professional safekeeping" in 2003, a decade after my finding of the microfilm at the Library of Congress.

Fortunately for readers and posterity, Blight's book and mine are different—indeed, complementary. Blight's book is a macronarrative built around two individuals whom Blight moves in and out of focus against the backdrop of the historiography of slavery and civil war. My book is a micronarrative, not unmindful of the larger context, but more concerned with the life and times of an urban, domestic slave in Fredericksburg and the white society surrounding him—more "thick description" than large theater. In my book, we get to see an antisecessionist, slaveholding flour miller; a family torn by antislavery and pro-Confederate sympathies; generational differences in attitudes towards slavery and war; rabid pro-Confederate men and women taking revenge against any who dared to disagree. And we see the different angles of vision, including those of slaves and free blacks, to the events swirling around them. Blight is not unaware of these tensions and conflicts, but he has not read the narratives of Jane Beale, Lizzie Alsop, the Blackford Minor family, or Moncure Conway, or researched the Southern Claims Commission Records for Spotsylvania and Stafford counties, where loyalty and dissent on the local level revealed the deep and lasting divisions and rifts war caused among families and friends.

Viewing this world through the eyes of John Washington for the first time was an unforgettable experience for me. I remember how close I felt to Washington and the places he was describing. Exactly a century apart in age, we trod over the same ground. The Brown farm was across the highway from my grandfather's house; the mill Washington describes was owned by a family that ran a country store where I used to enjoy Cokes and the local banter with my grandfather. Mount Pisgah Baptist Church was located in a place my family called "Tanners," an African American community in Madison County, five miles from Orange. For me, reading Washington's "Memorys" was like having an avatar move around the landscape of my own memories of rural Virginia and seeing it light up with Washington's words of description.

INTRODUCTION
Fredericksburg in 1838

John Washington's immediate surroundings in Spotsylvania County, Virginia, connect two regions, the Tidewater and the Piedmont, and Fredericksburg lies on one of the farthest western navigable points of the Rappahannock River. The Rappahannock derives its name from the Rappahannock Indians, who lived on the river when the English arrived in 1607. With its headwaters in the Blue Ridge Mountains, it traces a course extending for 105 miles from the mountains to the fall line, about 10 miles east of Fredericksburg, where it is joined by its chief tributary, the Rapidan River. From there it flows on into the coastal zone, draining the boggy estuaries that feed the Chesapeake Bay. In addition to the Rappahannock, three other rivers—the York, James, and Potomac—flow in a southeasterly direction from Virginia's interior and empty into the Chesapeake Bay, which in turn joins the Atlantic Ocean. On a map, the rivers look like large arteries with hairlike capillaries, and like capillaries they transmitted the materials and information that gave life to the region. The capillary-like streams east of the fall line drain into the main rivers that feed the heart of the Chesapeake Bay. Those waterways form the Tidewater region, oldest continuous Anglo-American settlement and, until emancipation, the deepest self-reproducing slave society in North America.

Tidewater, the land of the Cavaliers, is the name generally given to the "broad belt of undulating and river-gashed plain that borders the eastern seaboard of Virginia from the Potomac to the North Carolina line." Here the climate is mild and gentle—save for occasional hurricanes that visit the coast periodically—with about 258 days of sunshine, temperatures that average 40° in the winter and 80° in the summer, and an average growing season of 200 frost-free days. Closer to the bay, nineteenth-century newspaper ads for guano and other fertilizers reveal that black stiff and light sandy loam soils required heavy fertilization to grow crops. Farther east, farmers in areas of clay and sand loams practiced soil conservation, such as crop rotation and fallowing, to produce a wide variety of staple and regional crops, including wheat, transported downriver to be ground into flour; apples, to be pressed into cider; and tobacco, to be twisted into plugs, rolled into cigars, or pulverized into snuff.[1]

The Tidewater dissolves almost imperceptibly into the Piedmont region, which begins at the fall line and extends westward to the foothills of the picturesque Blue Ridge Mountains. The Virginia Piedmont broadens southward from a width of 40 miles at the north to about 185 miles at the North Carolina line. Channeling by streams has left few flat areas. Red clay hills and erosion-born ridges produce an undulating surface with altitudes ranging from about 300 feet in the east to heights as great as 2,200 feet at the base of the Blue Ridge. The Piedmont climate is slightly hotter and drier in summer and colder in the winter than that of the Tidewater. Limestone and clay soils produce bluegrass, grains, and fruits. As tobacco cultivation eventually impoverished Tidewater soils, Virginia's tobacco and slave culture began to move into the central and southern portions of the Piedmont. Spotsylvania County is evenly divided between Piedmont and Tidewater by the fall line, which runs through the middle of the county, passing just east of Fredericksburg.[2]

Spotsylvania County emerged as an early colonial frontier separating established homes and plantations in Virginia's Tidewater region from French and Indian encroachments on its western periphery. On 1 May 1721, Spotsylvania County's boundaries were fixed. In 1727, the General Assembly ordered that fifty acres of land in the county be laid out as a town to be named Fredericksburg for Frederick, the Prince of Wales and father of George III. The irony would be palpable to later residents, as Fredericksburg became a center of patriot activity in events leading up to the American Revolution. The earliest visitors to the area came by way of the river. Captain John Smith sailed up the tidewater part of the river to an island just below the falls at Falmouth, a small town situated across the Rappahannock River in Stafford County. In 1670, John Lederer explored and mapped the river north of the falls. In this general area, the towns of Falmouth, on the north side of the river near the falls, and Fredericksburg, on the south side of the river below the falls, came to be located. Lederer's map helped convince the General Assembly of the need for a fort in the vicinity of the falls. By 1680 settlement of the upper valley of the river had begun.[3]

Coastal ports like Norfolk, Portsmouth, and Baltimore provisioned the West Indies and southern Europe with farm products transported from the hinterlands of nearby river towns. River towns and coastal cities formed a nexus of riverine and oceanic trade. West Africa and the Caribbean had similar coastal networks. The great Atlantic Ocean was the common carrier, connecting the networks and slave cultures of Africa, the Caribbean, and Virginia. Ships left inland ports like Fredericksburg, for example, bearing a farmer's ear of corn from the Blue Ridge Mountains in Madison County bound for a planter's granary in Antigua. As early as 1762, perhaps sooner, the now-famous Kunta Kinte or Toby, his Americanized name, reached the plantation of William Waller, a Spotsylvania County physician. When the ships docked in Fredericksburg, local merchants—eager to sell their new inventories—quickly filled the newspapers, advertising their wares of salt, earthenware, coal, wooden casks, white lead, cheese, shot, spades and shovels, mustard, flannel, calico prints, furniture, Irish linen, tablecloths, Medoc Claret, sweet oil, olives, capers, anchovies, candles, soap, Antiguan rum, "Muscovado" sugar, and imperial tea. Ships regularly arrived and cleared the port of Fredericksburg. Even as late as 9 September 1840, for example, when canals, turnpikes, and railroads had diminished riverine traffic, arrivals included two schooners from Boston carrying salt; one schooner from Norfolk carrying sugar for local merchant T. F. Knox; another schooner from Richmond with coal; and the steamer *Rappahannock* from Baltimore with goods and sundries. Vessels clearing port included a schooner headed for Boston with flour and corn from Knox, and a schooner for New York with a load of wheat.[4]

The internal slave trade, too, was borne on the river; it had been so for at least two generations by the time Washington was born. The same local newspaper, for example, that advertised West Indian products for sale by Fredericksburg's merchants also carried the following announcement: "Servants for Sale. Will be sold, on Tuesday the 6th of February next, a valuable parcel of SERVANTS, late the property of Mrs. A. Lithgow, dec. The Sale at Buck's Auction Room.—Terms of Sale made known by the Auctioneer." Before the American Revolution, slave ships plied the waters of the Rappahannock as far north as Fredericksburg.[5]

In the aftermath of the post-1808 prohibition against the international slave trade, Fredericksburg's merchants participated in a vigorous inland traffic in slaves whose exact quantitative dimensions cannot be calculated. It was said that more slaves changed hands in side-alley trading-house deals than on the more visible public auction blocks. At the town's center, the rhythmic auctioneer's cry sometimes announced a quick sale to crowds of curious onlookers gathering in front of the Planters' Hotel, a three-and-a-half-story brick structure at the corner of William and Charles streets that was the focus of the public auction trade. Late in the war it served as a Union hospital. A stone block measuring two-and-a-half feet high and two feet wide—just wide enough to balance upon without falling off—still marks the spot in front of the hotel where slaves stood to be inspected and hired or sold at "public outcry." Tradition designated it a "horse block" that also functioned as a dais for slave auctions. As late as February 1862, the Planters' Hotel slave auction remained open.[6] Farther south, the area in front of the courthouse on Princess Anne Street was said to be still a third locale of slave auctions. Not even a century of time has been able to erase every vestige of the slave trade. Along the river, in the old tobacco warehouse district, physical evidence testifies to places where anxious slave arrivals or departures bound for Georgia, Alabama, Mississippi, and other areas of expanding plantation agriculture were held until boats came to transport them deeper into the South, from the darkness of a cell to a hell somewhere else on earth.[7] In the early 1970s, during an excavation to pave an office parking lot, workers discovered underground rooms measuring approximately eight by twelve feet, built of cobblestone, likely holding pens for slaves arriving or leaving. In 1850 approximately 1,200 slaves and 350 free blacks lived, worked, and mixed with white residents in the town.[8]

A northern visitor, Ethan Allen Andrews, writing in the summer of 1835, made some illuminating observations about the Fredericksburg slave market and its principal slave jail, which was the vantage point from which enslaved people contemplated sale and transport away from their families, friends, and the only society they knew. The jail in Fredericksburg, which resembled that of notorious Alexandria trader John Armfield, included an open-air courtyard partially enclosed by a wooden fence. Most likely, several jail cells opened on the courtyard, and slaves would be locked in the cells at night to sleep on a cobblestone floor. These could have been the underground cells found in the 1970s excavation. In the daylight and evening hours, enslaved people awaiting the journey from Fredericksburg took the last opportunity many of them had to relay news and sentiments to family and friends, as most would lose contact and never return. On the evening he visited the slave jail, Andrews "observed two or three negro women, from without, conversing through the fence with some who were confined in the yard, apparently cheerful and happy."[9] Perhaps the conversation was the last between friends or relatives, recalling joyful occasions past rather than speculating about the future. The slave market was often the last opportunity for loved ones to prevent family separation by intervening in sales. Andrews recalled such a situation.

Slave marriages were not safe from the intentions of slaveholders and slave traders, and even when outsiders intervened to keep enslaved spouses together, the slave market often destroyed marriages and scattered families. Andrews recalled that the "mistress" of an enslaved woman took "some offense at her, and had sold her to [a slave] trader, with the intention of having her carried out of the state." Not surprisingly, "The husband and wife were both greatly distressed." Upon hearing of the impending separation of the wife from her husband, a "gentleman" of Fredericksburg intervened, "and from compassion to them this gentleman purchased her." Despite the paternalistic interest of a white Fredericksburger, the couple was not safe. Andrews recalled that "after this trouble was over, a year or two passed quietly away, when the husband, who belonged to the minor heirs of an estate, was seized, just as a drove of negroes were setting off for the south, and immediately handcuffed to prevent his escape." Often, slaves did not become aware of impending separations or even sales until it was too late. Andrews continued, "He had been sold some time previously, but had not been informed of his fate, until the hour of departure arrived." In such cases, even intervention on the part of a concerned citizen was not sufficient. "The gentleman who had purchased the wife," Andrews recalled, "learning the circumstances, attempted to again prevent the separation of husband and wife, by offering to sell the latter to the trader, provided he would guarantee that they should not be separated, when sold at the south." In most cases, the current prices in the slave market, and not the bond of marriage, determined the fate of enslaved people sold away from each other. This situation was typical. "The trader was willing to purchase her," Andrews recalled, "but said he could give no such guaranty, as he always sold his slaves to those who would pay the highest price, and he supposed it possible, that for this purpose he should have to separate them."[10]

Although the circumstances differed, the outcome of these two situations was the same. In the first instance, the mistress of the wife had taken offense at something the wife may have done. In the second, the husband's owner died, and the husband was to be sold and the proceeds distributed to the owner's children according to the will. In both cases, an outsider intervened to stop the separation, but to no avail. Forced separation was the fate of approximately one in five of enslaved peoples' first marriages in the antebellum South.[11] The pain of family separation was often merely the beginning of the arduous journey south.

The slave trader using the Fredericksburg jail, according to Andrews, "is said to have about one hundred and fifty [enslaved people] on hand at this time, whom he is soon to send off, over land, I believe, to New Orleans."[12] The overland journey took place on often unmarked and poorly maintained dirt roads and through perilous river crossings. Attacks from wild animals were not infrequent. Many enslaved people died on the way of disease and exhaustion, some drowned crossing rivers, and pregnant mothers often died in childbirth. Men were usually chained together and forced to march—and sleep—in coffles. Women followed, while children, the elderly, and infirm slaves were usually transported in open carts, which often became mired in mud. Armed men on horseback watched closely. The one hundred and fifty slaves about whom Andrews heard were among approximately one million enslaved African Americans forcibly marched, shipped, or taken by railroad from the Upper South to the Lower South between 1790 and 1860. Two thirds of all emigrants were forced to move as a result of sale, and nearly two million more slaves were sold locally.[13] Despite observing that "the slaves were well dressed and clean," Andrews recalled that the slave trader who used the jail had recently engaged in the practice of "sending off a number of mothers without their little children, whom he had purchased with them." Andrews added that the trader had probably "separated them, because the children were of no value in the market to which the mothers were sent." A Pittsylvania County, Virginia, woman corroborated that observation. Fannie Berry recalled much later that "as soon as" young mothers who had just been sold "got on de train," the purchaser "had [the] train stopped an' made dem poor gal mothers take babies off and laid dem precious things on de groun' and left dem behind to live or die." Not all slaves sold from markets such as Fredericksburg would end up working on cotton or sugar plantations. Andrews was informed that "mulattoes are not so much valued for field hands," and consequently "they are purchased for domestics, and the females to be sold for prostitutes." "The latter fact I am sorry to state," Andrews sighed, adding that the "higher authority from which I received it forbids that it should be concealed."[14] It was into this world that John Washington, son of a white man and a slave woman, was born.

Ambiguities and contradictions have always abounded in the South, making it a region of striking contrasts that have bemused, beguiled, entertained, enraged, stumped, intrigued, fascinated, and bamboozled countless writers, scholars, musicians, newspaper editors, preachers, and others. Stop the clock in this small southern town, take a careful look around, and the most arresting phenomena were likely to be the paradoxes of southern life. New and old, aristocrat and commoner, merchant and plain-clothes farmers mixed together on Fredericksburg's streets in rituals of economic, social, and political discourse. Anachronistic social practices floated in a timeless suspension. Strutting, betting, and gaming, the playtime activities of aristocratic society, lingered at venues such as race courses, ballrooms, wine cellars, and sporting arenas. At wakes for the dead, slaves served drinks in containers with dark wrappings; wine was drunk "from glasses festooned with long black ribbons." Few could explain such curious protocols of social pretension then and now. Looking back, they seem even more anomalous for a nineteenth-century town devoted to modernizing.[15] On the rise, so it thought, Fredericksburg in 1840 boasted 73 stores, four semiweekly newspapers, roughly 4,000 inhabitants, and exports of approximately $4 million a year.

Spotsylvania and Stafford counties, with their largest towns of Fredericksburg and Falmouth, respectively, exhibited two different faces of the region. In the words of Stephen Ash, the region might be called a "third South," which like Middle Tennessee "gazed Janus-like toward the egalitarian, nonslaveholding South of the yeoman farmer and toward the plutocratic, plantation South," in this case the tobacco kings.[16] Spotsylvania County exhibited the features of traditional plantation agriculture while just across the Rappahannock River, Stafford County contained more small holdings. Spotsylvania had a black majority with 7,700 whites (1,031 of them slaveholders), 7,800 slaves, and 500 free blacks. Slaves and free blacks composed 45 percent of the region's total population but 52 percent of the county's population, which also had a higher concentration of wealth, fewer household heads, more slave owners, and a smaller number of free blacks. In Stafford County, slaves made up 39 percent of the population. A subsistence farming and fishing economy, Stafford had ten mills producing wheat and corn meal, and 70 percent of its manufacturing jobs were in shad and other fishing. When Lincoln visited in May 1862, Falmouth consisted of a church, a cotton factory, several brick storehouses, and numerous dwellings. A jail provided a place to hold the town miscreants and furnished a convenient service to slaveholders who could have their troublesome slaves flogged for $50 apiece. Mostly concentrated in Fredericksburg, Spotsylvania County's industry was largely carpentry; it accounted for the largest number of manufacturing jobs. Fredericksburg also had sizable numbers of merchants, shopkeepers, and artisans, even though its total population numbered 5,000 residents, 1,291 of them slaves.[17]

A traveler visiting Fredericksburg around the time of John Washington's birth would find a bustling village of several thousand inhabitants, a third of whom were slaves and free blacks. The town stood on the threshold of a prosperous future with its canal, railroad facilities, and river navigation by sailing vessels and steamboats. A few slaves lived in shacks on Sophia and lower Caroline streets in a declining shoreline area, where steamboats, schooners, brigs, and sloops tied up at the docks, wharves, and warehouses of merchants and shipowners. Little shops of coopers and blacksmiths nestled amid the chaos. An 1841 visitor found a town with mostly brick buildings, the result of previous fires. Public buildings included a courthouse, clerk's office, jail, market house, and orphan asylum. Denominational churches served Episcopal, Presbyterian, Methodist, Baptist, and Reformed Baptist congregations. Considerable grain, flour, and maize and quantities of gold were part of an annual export trade worth $4 million. There were 73 stores with capital of about $377,000: 2 tanneries, a paint store, a drug store, a grist mill, 2 printing offices, 4 newspapers, and capital of about $142,000 in manufacturing. Five academies served 256 students, seven schools enrolled 156 students, and one male and one female seminary admitted students "of the higher class." (Academies and seminaries typically taught a classier curriculum—classics, language, science, and history—while other schools taught reading, writing, and arithmetic.) Trade was mostly local, but Fredericksburg merchants carried on substantial business with the interior of the state extending beyond the Blue Ridge Mountains. It was not uncommon to see as many as 50–60 four- and six-horse teams from the interior in town at one time. A block west of Sophia Street—where Washington's mother lived in a small "shack" — and away from the river and warehouse area on Caroline Street, were the elegant homes of Fredericksburg's doctors, lawyers, merchants, and politicians. Two blocks farther west from the river on Princess Anne Street sat the homes of shopkeepers and artisans. In the center of town were the public buildings, schools, and churches. A visible free black community occupied the south of town. Slaves entered and exited Fredericksburg via a secret passageway running from their rural owners to town hirers.[18]

Despite Fredericksburg's vaunted role in Civil War history—the place where the Union suffered one of its worst defeats, or, from another vantage point, the place where the Confederacy won one of its most

View of Fredericksburg, Va., November 1862 (unscaled). Baltimore: E. Sachse & Co., 1863. From Library of Congress, Geography and Map Division.

glorious victories—Washington would have seen around him many who challenged slavery and war. Later he would locate on his personal map of the area (see appendix), some of those places where he had experienced freedom in various forms during his life in Fredericksburg. Even in an atmosphere where critical views of the South were unpopular, antebellum Fredericksburg was the home of leading antislavery figures and a surprising number of Unionists, who resisted the war and paid the price in the loss of friends, family hospitality, influence, and property.

Like the unnamed gentleman who intervened in the sales of husband and wife in the Fredericksburg slave market, Moncure Conway stood up against slavery, even though his position represented a small minority of white Virginians. Conway was a son of the Virginia aristocracy who became an abolitionist. According to his biographer, he was "successively Methodist minister, Unitarian minister, Theistic minister, freethought minister, no minister at all. . . . He was both a platform polemicist and a serious scholar whose biography of Thomas Paine is in many ways still the best." As this perceptive biographer states with admirable acumen, Conway came face to face with bloodshed, power, and authority in a fratricidal Civil War and reexamined the imperatives of an aristocratic family, organized Christianity, and the moral and political foundations of a slave society.[19] Mary Minor Blackford was also from an aristocratic family and an avid antislavery figure. A loyal member of the American Colonization Society, Blackford was intense and unrelenting in her hatred of slavery. She and her family deplored the excesses of the rabid southern secessionists and supported the Union until Lincoln's call for 75,000 troops following the attack on Fort Sumter forced them to choose sides. Thereafter the family supported the Confederacy, though Mary never lost her distaste for slavery. Other Unionists also took courageous and unpopular stands, like Conway's and Blackford's, and wealth insulated them from the consequences of public disapproval. Others were not so lucky. The Rev. James W. Hunnicutt, editor of the *Christian Banner,* a Free Will Baptist, and an avid Unionist, whose position made him a pariah of Fredericksburg, had to suspend publication of the *Banner* in May 1861 because secessionists threatened his life.[20]

Citizens who stood against slavery were joined by those who stood for the Union during the Civil War. As we shall see later, local merchant-miller Joseph C. Ficklin never wavered in his unionism from the moment he defied the poll watchers—secessionist partisans who tried to intimidate voters during Virginia's secession vote of 1861—and refused to have his vote characterized as pro-secession and on through the war years, when he protected his sons from the Confederate draft by sneaking them through enemy lines to the North. As the records of the Southern Claims Commission reveal, unionism remained strong in Fredericksburg throughout the Civil War, and its followers constituted a kind of semiclandestine community of believers who knew and supported one another, took great risks in holding their position, and at times had to flee north for their safety.[21]

Free blacks also stuck together, supported one another, and sought self-improvement through apprenticeships, indentured service, and political activism. Many had used literacy to gain their freedom from slavery. Drawn to towns like Fredericksburg with its opportunities for artisans and a variety of labor needs, free blacks continued to use the advantages of literacy to improve themselves. No doubt they inspired slaves like Washington as well.

African Americans in Fredericksburg did not rely on whites to guide them in their quest to gain literacy, as the example of Noah Davis illustrates. Noah Davis understood literacy in terms of the Frederick Douglass model. Born in nearby Madison County in 1804, Davis together with his family belonged to Robert Patton, son-in-law of Revolutionary War hero Hugh Mercer and a wealthy merchant from Scotland who owned property in several Virginia counties. Patton lived near the falls above Fredericksburg and was known as "one of the noblest, most upright, most generous men." Using the Bible as his tool, Davis taught himself and later his own children to read and write, and wrote his autobiography. In 1818, the 14-year-old Davis left Madison County for Fredericksburg. He described it as an occasion whose sadness was mitigated by the reputation of Fredericksburg as "the greatest place in the world." He arrived after a wagon trip of a day and a half, "a boy green from the country . . . astonished and delighted at what appeared to me the splendor and beauty of the place."[22]

Davis was bound out to Thomas Wright for approximately six years, until he reached the age of twenty-one, to learn the boot- and shoe-making trade. All of Wright's indentures were required to serve a year with his wife in the house and kitchen so that when called from the shop they could serve as waiters or cooks. Fredericksburg's shoemakers had the reputation as "the most intemperate of any class of men in the place." As a journeyman, Davis had the duty of secretly bringing liquor to the men without the knowledge of the boss, who forbade it in the shop.[23]

In 1838, a group representing themselves as "free people of color residing in the Corporation of Fredericksburg and natives of the State of Virginia" petitioned the General Assembly for permission to open a school. Appealing initially to the state's sense of honor and duty, they described themselves variously as descendants of soldiers of the Revolutionary War and the War of 1812. Then, sounding one of the themes of Reconstruction much later, they got to the heart of their petition about the consequences of denying an education in a society increasingly based upon knowledge. "Those persons who are so unfortunate as not to be in some slight degree educated," they complained, "are cut off from the ordinary means of self-advancement and find the greatest difficulty in gaining an honest livelihood." They pointed out that it was necessary for them to send their children to the North for an education, at great expense. They requested that "an act be passed authorizing a school in the Corporation of Fredericksburg, for the instruction of the free people of color therein." The legislature disagreed, of course, and refused to grant the petition, ironically citing an 1831 statute to prohibit meetings of free blacks for the purpose of education.[24] Meeting this resistance, the free black inhabitants of the town, led by the DeBaptist family, organized a migration to Detroit, Michigan.

Fredericksburg's free black community understood literacy neither exclusively in the Frederick Douglass sense of illiteracy as a mark of slavery, ignorance, and inelegance nor entirely, as we shall see, in the Sojourner Truth/John Washington context of literacy as an alternative way of knowing or "reading" one's enemies through careful observation and analysis. Rather, free persons of color in Fredericksburg sounded a modern note, like Booker T. Washington, linking education to skill development and upward mobility, an understanding quite sophisticated for its place (a small southern town) and time (prior to the advent of labor differentiation associated with industrialization).[25]

Washington's recollections support the Sojourner Truth understanding of literacy, not that of Fredericksburg's free black community. For Washington, learning to read and write were essential steps on the ladder to freedom. Freedom had to be gained, sometimes seized, other times negotiated, and was usually gotten by outfoxing owners and other whites. Skills of reading and writing were the necessary tools of freedom. Washington took every opportunity to gain literacy. He managed to get help in spelling from two whites in the Farmers' Bank, where he worked as a slave. His mother made him a copy of the alphabet. He secured additional help from a free mulatto painter and paper hanger who was working in the bank and secretly made him a good copy of the alphabet.

A bright, literate slave of great sensitivity to the world around him, John Washington was undoubtedly well aware of the divisions within the white political community. These differences likely stirred the winds of freedom that encouraged a man like Washington to be bold and emancipate himself.

NOTE ON EDITORIAL METHOD

John Washington is at the center of this book. I have transcribed his narrative and run it first with his own chapter breaks. My annotations of explanation and historical context follow Washington's recollections in a section entitled "Comments on Chapter 1," and so on, at the end of each chapter. Asterisks mark passages in the narrative that are annotated. Contemporary diaries, local histories, public records, manuscript collections, and scholarly works guide the annotations and provide supporting evidence for Washington's recollections, which prove admirably accurate and informed.

Editing has been kept to a minimum. Chapter titles 1 through 5 are those given by John Washington. He did not title chapters 6 through 11. I have chosen titles for these chapters based upon the central theme or event covered in each and my own sense of what words Washington might have used to capture the essence of this part of his life. Words appear as he spelled them, and only when it seems necessary to avoid misunderstanding is the word *sic* used. Quotation marks are reproduced as in the original—sometimes only at the beginning or end of direct speech, sometimes around such phrases as "he replied" rather than around the actual quoted material. Paragraph breaks, insofar as they could be determined, remain the same as in the original handwritten version.

John Washington's Civil War

Childhood

I Was born (in Fredericksburg Virginia: May 20th 1838.) a Slave to one Thomas R. Ware Sr.* who I never had the pleasure of knowing, (I Suppose it Might have been a doubtful pleasure.) as he died before I was born. When I was about 2 years of age My Mother (who was also a Slave) was hired to one Richard L. Brown* in Orange County Virginia, about 37 miles from Fredericksburg, and I was taken along with her. But I will not promise to narate the incidents of that Jurney as I did not keep a Diary at that age in a Slave State.* My reccolections of my early childhood has been no doubt the most plasant of my life. My Mother taught me to spell at a very early age (between 4 years and 8)

When at this time of Life I look back to that time and, all its most vivid reccolections I see Myself a Small light haired boy (very often passing easily for a white boy.)* playing Mostly with the white children on the farm, in Summers Evening among the Sweet-Scented cloverfields after the Butterflys Wading the Brooks and with pin hook and line Startling the finny life.

Now in the Great Forrest Surrounded with dogs in quest of the Hare and Opossum, often on the top of Some Neighbouring Mountain trying with My young eyes, to get a View of Fredericksburg in the distant about 37 Miles Eastward, The View from all points was splendid, the Westward View, North and Northwest a few Miles distant was the "Blue Ridge Mountins," But still nearer was the Rappid Ann River 3 miles distant, the nearest ford being "Willis' Mills,"* where I used to Stand and Wonder at the River Damed over, and the Great Old Moss covered Wheel Slowly revolving and throwing the Water off in beautiful Showers.

And Orange Court House, where I was carried once behind the family careage, along with the White children to see a Circus. And in the great Crowd during a Violent Thunder Storm I was lost. and the carrage arrived at home Without me. and Mother and all thought I had fallen asleep in My Seat behind the carrage and and [sic] been washed off in the "Mountain Run," which was very high and had to be forded, by the horses.

I Wanderd about the Street at the Court House. (there was but one

Street) until dark and I had began to Cry and Wonder Where I should Sleep, for I did not know any one in the village, and could not think what I should do. and the crowds of Country people were clearing the place very rappidly

When all at once My Godmother found me* and soon had me Safely packed away amoung a lot of Comforts and Countelpins [comforters and counterpanes?] in an Old Lumbering ox cart going to the Next farm to my home. When I arrived safe at about Sunlite next Morning. Amidst great rejoicing.

A Man was just getting ready to come and look for me. I was never allowed to go to another Circus at Orange Court House.

Once in a Month there used to [be] Meetings held for Divine Services (on the 4th Sundays I think) at "Mount Pisgah" Meeting house Situated on the East end of the farm Where Two Roads intersected. I know they were "Baptists," because the[y] used to Baptize in the Creek close by.

To these Meetings Mother hardly Ever failed to attend and take me with her, the church a Large frame building with Gallerys around for colord people to Sit in. Tall pine trees Surrounded the building and the horses and mules used to be fastened during the Services.

Cakes, Candy and fruits, used to be Sold there under those great pine trees, on Sundays; which, to my Eyes was always a great treat. I loved very much to go to the Meeting House, as it was called then, because I never failed to come home With a load of cakes candy and .c [etc.].

These are my first reccolections of attending a church and to-day in my 35th year the Memory is bright as events of to-day.*

Minute events of my reccolection will not likely interest you, So I must pass on with a glance at some of the Most important events.

Very early in my infantcy Mother taught me that Memorable little childs prayer not yet forgotten:

"Now I lay me down to sleep"*
I pray the lord my Soul to Keep"

and then the "Lords Prayer" when I got older.

The Usual Routine of farm work went on for a long time (it seemed to me).

The slaves were treated kindly,* and every Sunday Morning the weeks Rations were issued to them from the great meal house.

Harvest time a festival of pies and Meats fruits and vegitables would be Set out* in the yard on a great table in the Shade and the reapers and binders, Men and Women Seemed So happy merry and free, for whiskey was not Withheld by the "Boss."

And then hog killing time (near Christmas)* when great fires were kindled and large Stones made red hot, then placed into great hogsheads of water until it boiled for Scalding the hogs. and Every body was bussy, noisey and merry. Every one of the Slaves were permitted to raise their own hogs, and fowls, and had a garden of their own from the Eldest Man to Me—

often at night Singing and dancing, prayer Meeting or corn Shucking.

"A corn shucking" is always a Most lively time among the Slaves, they would come for miles around to join in Singing, Shouting and yelling as only a Negro can yell, for a good Supply of Bad Whiskey, corn Bread and Bacon and cabbage.*

At Christmas time Slaves were furnished with their new cloths Hats or Caps Boots and Shoes.

From the oldest to the little children they would be Summonsed to the "great House," as they called it (the owners) and each Man and Woman would receive their Christmas gift namely Flour, Sugar, Whiskey, Molases etc. according to the number in the family and they would go to their "cabins" and for the next six days have a holiday,* and make thing lively with Egg-nogg, Opossum, Rabbit, Coons and Everything of the kind.

COMMENTS ON CHAPTER 1

I Was born (in Fredericksburg Virginia: May 20th 1838.) a Slave to one Thomas R. Ware Sr. Catherine Ware, age forty-eight, owned no real estate in Spotsylvania County in 1838. Her two sons, Thomas R. Ware, Jr., twenty-three, and William Ware, eighteen, probably lived with her. Much later, in 1860, when the census enumerator visited the home of Catherine Taliaferro (Catherine had married Frank Taliaferro after Ware's death and he, too, had died by 1860), he found her two sons still living with her in the household: Thomas R. Ware, Jr., now forty-five, a "purser" in the U.S. Navy, and his brother William Ware, now forty, a teller at Farmers' Bank. The 1860 census showed Catherine with personal property valued at $5,500 with seven slaves in Fredericksburg: a 65-year-old mulatto female, a 37-year-old mulatto female, a 22-year-old mulatto male, an 11-year-old mulatto female, a 9-year-old mulatto male, a 6-year-old mulatto female, and a 2-year-old mulatto female.[1] But this underestimates her wealth because the census account does not include John Washington, his mother, and his four brothers and sisters, not living in the household.

As we will see, the slave populations in other Fredericksburg households were likewise characterized by substantial numbers of mulattoes, indicating a high rate of interracial mixing, a feature of urban slavery in general.[2]

My Mother (who was also a Slave) was hired to one Richard L. Brown. Unfortunately, a search of census records failed to turn up a Richard L. Brown.[3]

Washington's narrative provides some intriguing windows on slave domestic life. His recollections never mention his mother by name; usually he refers to her as "My Mother" or simply "Mother." It was not unusual for southern children to avoid use of the actual names of their parents or to ignore fathers. After all, women did play a much larger role in the domestic life of southern children, free and slave, black and white, than men. Nor would it have been unusual for Washington to be indifferent to his father's identity. The primary responsibility for child care and rearing fell almost exclusively to women in both white and slave households. Consequently, children, especially slave children—who often had no other person to fall back upon except their own mother—developed extremely close bonds to their mothers and weak or even nonexistent ties with fathers. The absence of reference to Washington's father anywhere in the recollections is curious, however, and may mean any of several things: Washington never knew who his father was; he knew his father was a white man, and the subject of interracial sex was taboo; or it was just not important to him to learn his father's identity because his father had never been around him.

I did not keep a Diary at that age in a Slave State. Keeping a diary, a harmless practice for any white person and scarcely worthy of comment, was an act of defiance for both free blacks and slaves who lived in Virginia in the post–Nat Turner era. As one historian has observed, educated people of the nineteenth century viewed literacy as a "signifier of modernity" and reading as "the best means of acquiring knowledge." After Turner's infamous revolt of 1831, a distance just over 120 miles from Fredericksburg Courthouse, planters viewed reading and writing as a dangerous literacy. An 1831 statute declared that "all meetings of free Negroes or mulattoes, at any school house, church meeting house, or any other place for teaching them reading and writing . . . shall be deemed . . . an unlawful assembly." As in the case of much statutory law dealing with slavery, literacy laws actually policed white behavior. According to the 1860 Code of Virginia: "If a white person assemble with negroes for the purpose of instructing them to read or write . . . he shall be confined in jail not exceeding six months and fined not exceeding one hundred dollars."[4] White prohibitions against black literacy grew out of the needs for authority and control. Freedom and equity molded black understandings of literacy, but free blacks and slaves differed on the means to achieve freedom through literacy. In these differences, we can find the seeds of the end-of-the-century debate between Booker T. Washington and W. E. B. Du Bois over literacy and education.

I see Myself a Small light haired boy (very often passing easily for a white boy.) Washington's report of his complexion indicates that his father was probably white.[5] Indeed, he might have been the son of Thomas R. Ware, Sr., although no evidence of his paternity exists. What difference did his mulatto status make in his life? His lighter skin color is probably not the explanation for interracial play. It was not uncommon for slaves, regardless of complexion, to play with white children until about eight to ten years of age, when they entered the fields or became domestic laborers. The offspring of interracial unions sometimes did receive preferential treatment, however. Mulattoes, for example, might be shielded from harsh punishments or the hard labor of field hands, especially by planters with a special interest in their slave offspring. In his case, Washington's status as a domestic servant is suggestive of favoritism. Unlike his mother, who was hired out as a field hand, Washington remained a house slave for most of his life, except for the short periods when he was hired out to other masters. His surname is also indicative though not conclusive proof of preferential treatment, since slaves typically were known by their first names alone. It is not entirely clear what exactly, whether racial or circumstantial considerations, shaped his particular life course in slavery.

Still nearer was the Rappid Ann River 3 miles distant, the nearest ford being "Willis' Mills." Where I grew up, a hundred years after John Washington, just across the road from my grandfather's house was a large farm owned by Ralph Brown. About two miles away was the Rapidan River and the site of T. O. Gillum's Mill with an old, moss-covered, dormant wheel. After a century, the name of the mill may have changed, but these may be the same sites or certainly ones very similar to those to which Washington refers. Orange Court House was about five miles away. It was the county seat of Orange County, founded on land taken from neighboring Spotsylvania County in 1734 and named for the son-in-law of George II of Britain, Prince William IV of Orange. In Washington's day, slaves accounted for 59 percent of a total population of just over 10,000 people in Orange County.[6] Orange Court House was the focus of local wheat and tobacco production because of railroad lines that connected it with the port city of Alexandria, Virginia.

All at once My Godmother found me. Nothing indicates the identity of this "Godmother." Who was this angel of mercy who recognized Washington and made arrangements for him to be transported home safely? It might have been a grandmother or an aunt, both of whom he later mentions. It might have been a kind white woman who knew the family. Perhaps it was a woman of color, free or slave, who understood the predicament of a young slave boy lost in an unfamiliar town.

These are my first reccolections of attending a church and to-day in my 35th year the Memory is bright as events of to-day. The report of Washington's age establishes 1872 or 1873 as the year the recollections were recorded. These memories of attending church on Brown's farm and general feelings about religion contrast sharply with his later attitudes and behavior in Fredericksburg. Part of the difference is undoubtedly due to a nostalgia which customarily attaches to many early childhood experiences. Washington recalls life as a child before the responsibilities of labor. He distinguishes this very brief pre-slave age in his life by entitling this chapter of his narrative "Childhood." He was free to play with white children, to roam about, and had yet to comprehend the owner's use of religion as a means of social control. But it is not just nostalgia that Washington conveys in his recollections about early childhood.

Washington evokes the world of slavery during his youth in unmistakable terms. It is in these recollections that he provides readers with his earliest impressions of slavery. The events he recalls with such passion and vividness conjure up, not the paternal master-slave relationship nor solely slavery's degradations, but metaphorical images of the slave community itself. That Washington's warmest and fondest memories are of the slave community and its intimacies confirms how slaves found the means to defeat becoming a mere object of the slaveholder's will via family break-up, naming practices, forced religion, or other means of social control which masters sought to impose. Slaves strove to keep families together, called one another by their own names in secret, and reconfigured the slaveholders' Christianity into a theology of emancipation. Here, for example, Washington's recollections include summer picnics under cool pine trees, baptisms in the creek, and feasts of sweets and baked goods, each of which conjures up memories of slave gatherings.[7]

"Now I lay me down to sleep." The intimate bond between Washington and his mother is evident here when he records as the first "important event" his mother's teaching of this well-known child's prayer.

The slaves were treated kindly. Unlike planters, Washington did not esteem physical treatment, especially as it entails the provision of food, clothing, and shelter, to be the true measure of his slave experience, whether benign or cruel. Generally, the context of physical treatment was bound to masters' understandings of discipline and control and quite at variance with slave attitudes. To make material needs the measure of slavery, as slaves understood, trivialized liberty and vulgarized life itself. As Thomas Wentworth Higginson, a northern antislavery leader who led a black regiment during the Civil War, noted: "It was not the individuals, but the ownership of which they complained. That they saw to be a wrong which no special kindnesses could right." A staple of cornmeal and bacon, coarse clothes, and cold, dank, and drafty quarters, although more than an annoyance, were inconsequential to slaves when compared to the blessings of freedom.[8]

Slavery had matured since the Colonial Age; it was now more give and take. One observer has captured day-to-day master-slave relations eloquently, noting that at the heart of all daily encounters was the contest for advantage incessantly pursued, "sometimes noisily, more often quietly; sometimes violently, more often surreptitiously; infrequently with arms, always with the weapons of the mind and soul."[9]

Harvest time a festival of pies and Meats fruits and vegitables would be Set out. Virginia slaves were used primarily in wheat and corn cultivation, but during the winter months they were employed in other seasonal work, such as preserving meat and grains, tending winter gardens, clearing fallow or overgrown fields, mending fences, and maintaining irrigation and drainage systems.[10] Harvest festivals stimulated warm feelings of community among the slaves while they served simultaneously the master's bargaining power to demand more from the slaves as repayment for his kindness.

And then hog killing time (near Christmas). These recollections reflect the agricultural rhythms of the hog and corn culture most common to rural Virginia. Corn was usually harvested and the ears fed to hogs to fatten them just prior to butchering. With no artificial refrigeration, "hog-killin' time" required several days of cold weather, long enough to preserve the meat until the salt and smoke could take effect. Late November or early December usually provided the necessary cold spell in Virginia. The day of hog killing was a hustle-bustle of activity. Labor was divided: Some killed the hogs (usually by gunshot or by simply catching them and cutting their throats), others built fires for the large water pans, still others scalded the hogs so the hair could be scraped off. The carcasses were then hung on a pole or laid out for workers to cut up the meat. Women in the kitchen would be busy rendering fat to use in making soap, grinding scraps into sausage, or cooking fresh meat and other foods to feed the hungry butchers. The hams, shoulders, and sides would be packed in salt and pepper for about three months, after which the meat was "cured." Any portions that failed to cure would simply be cut out and thrown away. The pieces were hung up in the "meathouse" to keep animals from getting at them. At this stage the pork might also be smoked by building a smothered fire in the house. Washington indicates that slaves were allowed to raise their own hogs. Presumably, hog killing combined the animals of both masters and slaves.

Singing, Shouting and yelling as only a Negro can yell, for a good Supply of Bad Whiskey, corn Bread and Bacon and cabbage. Washington reveals here that he is not unaware that masters used these occasions to curry the favor of slaves. Some slaveholders encouraged overindulgence as a ploy to get slaves through the holidays and ready for winter work. Frederick Douglass recalled that during the Christmas holidays some slaves "would employ themselves in making corn-brooms, mats, horse-collars, and baskets; and another class of us would spend the time in hunting opossums, hares, and coons." He recalled, however, that "by far the larger part engaged in such sports and merriments as playing ball, wrestling, running foot-races, fiddling, dancing, and drinking whisky; and this latter mode of spending the time was by far the most agreeable to the feelings of our masters." Douglass contended that slaveholders used whiskey in particular to keep slaves from thinking about earning money through independent industry lest they do so in the hopes of buying their freedom—or running away.[11] Based on his own experience, he believed "these holidays to be among the most effective means, in the hands of slaveholders, of keeping down the spirit of insurrection among the slaves."[12]

Each Man and Woman would receive their Christmas gift . . . and they would go to their "cabins" and for the next six days have a holiday. Corn shuckings, hog killing, and Christmastime were three occasions for feasting on the plantation, "the first an immovable one but the last two . . . movable feasts in the African almanac," according to one planter. Masters deceived themselves when they encouraged slaves to "play the happy darkie" and then interpreted their singing and dancing as signs of satisfaction with their masters and their lives as slaves.[13] Slaves on many plantations engaged in yearly jollification, "Jubilee beating," which included costumed performances in which slaves could criticize masters and demand payment for their effort. Slaveholders happily obliged. Douglass recalled that "almost every farm has its 'Juba' beater. The performer improvises as he beats, and sings his merry songs, so ordering the words as to have them fall pat with the movement of his hands. Among a mass of nonsense and wild frolic, once in a while a sharp hit is given to the meanness of slaveholders."[14]

From the slaves' point of view, in Washington's recollections, these were celebrations of community and freedom, despite the transparency of the owners' intentions. They were times of reflection on the year passing away and times to make plans for the year ahead. Although planters could and did intrude, these were occasions where slaves escaped from some of the rigor of plantation discipline and oversight. The events often provided an opportunity to melt into the population, especially in corn shuckings, as slaves comingled with those from several different plantations. Many slaves got to visit kin—often husbands and wives—who resided some distance away. Others who had been hired out often returned, as hiring fairs took place after Christmas. Sumptuous meals also accompanied these festivals. Whether they came together for shucking corn or butchering hogs, the large numbers, the anonymity of being on a strange plantation, and the variety of the tasks made for greater freedom, at least temporarily. Similarly, at Christmastime planters typically gave slaves time off from regular duties in addition to extra rations, including liberal allotments of whiskey. Consequently these were times of gayety and élan, something that broke the dull, monotonous routine and gave slaves a chance to enjoy themselves as a large community.

2

Slavery

At about 4 years of age Mother learned me the alphabet* from the "New York Primer." I was kept at my lessons an hour or Two each night by My Mother;

My first great Sorrow was caused by Seeing one Morning, a number of the "Plantation Hands," formed into line, with little Bundles Straped to their backs, Men, Women and children. and all Marched off to be Sold South,* away from all that was near and dear to them, Parents, Wives husbounds and children; all Separated one from another, perhaps never to meet again on Earth.

I Shall never forget the weeping that Morning amoung those that were left behind, each one expecting to go next.

It was not long before all on that farm was doomed to the Same fate.

and those that did not belong to the "Planter" had to be sent home to their owner. The farm, and farming implements, Stock and everything was Sold. and Mr Brown removed to western Virginia.

Mother with me and four other *children [footnote in original: *Louisa, Laura, Georgianna and Willie] was sent to Fredericksburg Va. where we all arrived safe after 2 days travel in an Old "Road Wagon," Soon there after My Mother was sent to live to herself, that is to earn her own, and four little children's living without any help from our owners (except) Doctors Bills.

Poor Mother struggled hard late and early to get a poor pittance for the children all of which was to Small to help her. I was kept at the house of the "Old Mistress,"* all day to run erands and wait on the table (or any thing else that I could do.

N.B. At this time (the fall of 1848) Mrs Taliaferro our old mistress, she haveing married a Mr Frank Taliaferro who had since died, boarded at the "Farmers Bank,"* N.W. cor. of George and Princess Ann Streets. Mother lived in a little house on George St. Bet. Sophia St. and the River.

I was dressed every Morning (except) Sunday in a neat white Apron and clean Jacket and Pants and Sent up to the Bank to see What Mistress might want me to do. Possibley She would have nothing at al for me to do, and if So, I would be ordered to sit down on a footstool, in her room for hours at a time when other children of My age would be out at play.

On Sundays I was dressed in my Sunday cloths (without the Apron) and Sent to the Baptist Church,* cor Hanover and Sophia Sts of which the old Mistress was a Strict member. I used to have to sit where the old Lady could see me.

As proff that I was there atal at that time the White and Colord occupied the Same Church. Only all the slave colord Sat in the gallery on each Side, and the free colored Sat in the gallery fronting the Pulpit.

In the Afternoon of Sundays the Colored People used to have Meetings in the Basement of the church. to which I was regularly Sent and and [sic] Ordered, to bring home the text in Order that the Old Mistress might know whether I had been there or not.

Now the result of all this compulsinary church attending was just the reverse of What was desired* viz: I became a thourough hater of this Church and consequently, I resorted to all kinds of Subtirfuge imaginable to Stay away from Church.

I Would go to the church door and there wait, until the Minister would announce his text then commit it to Memory, So I could tell When I went home. This No Sooner done than I would hasten off to the river to play with Some boat or Other, Which I could always get or to Swim or play Marbles or, any thing in Preference to Sitting in church.

I Soon became a confirmed Liar: on account of being compelled to go to Church. TOO MUCH that one Church, I was scarcely ever allowed to go elsewhere.

COMMENTS ON CHAPTER 2

At about 4 years of age Mother learned me the alphabet. Undoubtedly with the benefit of hindsight, Washington realized in 1872 how important literacy had been to his escape from slavery. Ultimately he would build upon these early teachings by a loving mother to become literate and, like Frederick Douglass, use the knowledge that literacy gave him to good advantage in dealing with his owners, eventually emancipating himself.

My first great Sorrow was caused by Seeing one Morning, a number of the "Plantation Hands" . . . Marched off to be Sold South. Slavery dawned early in the memory of John Washington. Hardly has the narrative begun before he concludes his chapter on childhood and begins to write about slavery. He associates his "first great sorrow" with a slave sale and the break-up of slave families. Understandably, the sight of families being separated shocked the young boy. Later he would be separated from his own mother with great emotional impact. "Social death" or "natal alienation" is what one scholar has called it, a process of detachment of the slave from his own family roots and kinship community. After 1808 and the closing of the Atlantic slave trade to America, planters began to practice "amelioration," i.e., they encouraged the natural increase of the slave population, a process one historian called "domestication." The internal slave trade, however, probably robbed these practices of whatever pacifying effects might otherwise have obtained. In fact, the interstate slave trade thrived with the westward expansion. It is estimated that between 1800 and 1860, 800,000 slaves moved from east to west; Virginia alone exported approximately 483,000 slaves during this period, a number greater than that of the entire state population of approximately 472,500 slaves in 1860. Pacification of the slave populations in the South took on even greater significance after one of the bloodiest revolts in North American slave history. In 1831 Nat Turner led a slave rebellion in Virginia that killed sixty whites, many as they slept in their beds.[1]

I was kept at the house of the "Old Mistress." Apparently Mrs. Taliaferro had bought the whole family but used only John as her personal slave. The rest of the family, while not free, had to care for themselves. Later she would hire the entire family out. Hiring out slaves was a common practice in the antebellum period. Washington often referred to his owner as the "old mistress," rather than by her name, indicating a lack of respect for her. Other whites, for whom he had more respect, he addressed formally.

Mrs Taliaferro our old mistress . . . boarded at the "Farmers Bank." The Farmers' Bank was a two-story brick structure that housed both the Taliaferro-Ware residence and the Fredericksburg branch of the Farmers' Bank of Virginia. It included two dependencies: a brick kitchen and probably a slave quarter nearby, likely the place where Washington stayed when he was not with his mother. The bank was located on the northwest corner of George and Princess Anne streets.[2]

On Sundays I was dressed in my Sunday cloths . . . and Sent to the Baptist Church. At 801 Sophia Street was the Fredericksburg Baptist Church, which was located near the riverfront just two blocks over from where Catherine Taliaferro lived, at 900 Princess Anne Street. Up to 1854, it was a white church with slave and free black members. When white Baptists built elsewhere in 1854, the church was sold to black Baptists and renamed the African Baptist Church (see map), of which John Washington was recorded as a member.[3] Before the Civil War, whites retained control through George Rowe, a white minister. During the war it became a hospital, and after some repairs it took the name Shiloh. In 1860, Rowe owned at least four slaves in Fredericksburg: a 10-year-old mulatto female, a 6-year-old mulatto male, a 2-year-old mulatto male, and an 8-month-old mulatto female.[4]

Now the result of all this compulsinary church attending was just the reverse of What was desired. Slave religion has been the object of extensive inquiry. As historians have demonstrated, slave religion was a blend of African and African American traditions forged in the slave communal environment during after-work hours, and carried forth into the workplace as a source of strength and resistance. Slaves rejected the owners' narrow version of Christianity and its one-dimensional message of obedience and docility. Instead, they blended their own cultural heritage of African religion with conventional beliefs and what might be called "emancipation theology." In their after-hours "praise meetings," occasions of unrestrained emotion and communal affirmation, slaves prayed for deliverance, sang songs of sorrow and hope, and preached messages of deliverance and freedom. Using a structure of "call and response" in both sermons and spirituals and concluding with the "shout" dance, slaves translated the meaning of their experience into their own language and blended traditional African customs with Christianity.[5]

If Catherine Taliaferro hoped to use religion as a means of social control, it is obvious from Washington's response that her efforts failed. Instead he took advantage of her delusions to seize additional freedom for himself.

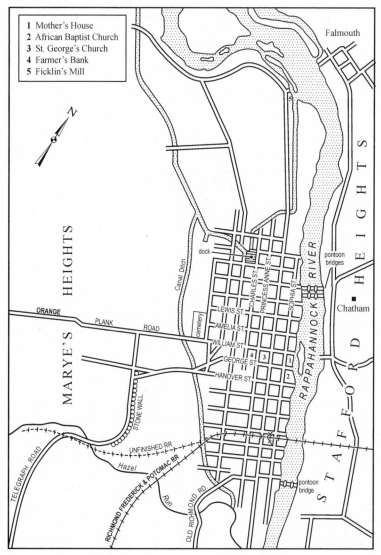

Street map of Fredericksburg, adapted from *The Journal of Jane Howison Beale of Fredericksburg, Virginia, 1850–1862* (Fredericksburg, Va.: Historic Fredericksburg, printed under the direction of Barbara Willis, 1979), 28. Redrawn by Mary Lee Eggart.

3

Left Alone

I had now arrived at the age of between 11 and 12 years [that is, 1849 or 1850], and had began to See Some of the many trials of Slavery.

Mother lived alone and maintained us children for about 2 years, perhaps, When Mrs Taliaferro came to the conclusion that Mother with My Sisters Louisa, Laura, Georgianna, and brother Willie would have to be sent to Staunton Virginia, to be hired to one R. H. Phillips.

Accordingly they were, all fitted out with New dresses, Shoes and Bonnetts, With Mothers bed cloths and some other few articles, and then was in readiness for their long jurney across the Blue Ridge Mountins in the month of December 1850 about Christmas.

The Night before Mother left me (as I was to be kept in hand by the Old Mistriss for especial use) She, Mother, came up to my little room I slept in the "white peoples house," and laid down on my Bed by me and begged me for her own sake, try and be a good boy, Say my Prayers every Night, remember all she had tried to teach me, and always think of her.

her tears mingled with mine amid kisses and heart felt Sorrow. She tucked the Bed cloths around me, and bade me good night.

Bitter pangs filled my heart and thought I would rather die, on the Morrow Mother and Sisters and Brother all would leave me alone in this Wide world to battle with temptation, trials and hardships.

Who then could I complain to When I was persecuted; who then Would come early the cold winter Mornings and call me up and help me do my hard tasks?

whose hand (patting) me upon the head would sooth my early trials.

Then and there My hatred was kindled Secretly against my oppressors, and I promised Myself If ever I got an opporteunity I would run away from these devilish Slave holders. The Morrow came and with tears and Lamentations cars left with all that was near and dear to me on Earth.*

A Week afterwards I heard they had all arrived safe in Staunton.

We Wrote often to each other as circumstances Would admit. Of Course, the White people had to write and read all the letters that passed between us. About this time I began seriously to feel the need of learn to write for Myself. I took advantage of every opporteunity to improve in Spelling. I had to attend to cleaning Mr. William Wares Room and he kept a large quanity of Books on hand amoung them "Harpers New Monthly Magazine," I used to take much pleasure in reading (but imperfectly) Short Stories, which soon induced me to look for the Book with lively interest each month. Two young Men (white) used to sleep with Mr Wm Ware of nights, named Roberts and they assisted me very much in Spelling only.

For it positively [was] forbiden by law to teach a Negro to Wrote, So I had to fall back upon my own resources.*

COMMENTS ON CHAPTER 3

The Morrow came and with tears and Lamentations cars left with all that was near and dear to me on Earth. For the second time, Washington experiences family break-up, the previous time being on the Brown plantation when he is just four years old. This time it affects him personally and even more deeply and brings back the bad memories of family separations he witnessed on the plantation. These family break-ups were unquestionably the most momentous events of his life, and more than any other feature of slavery, they burnish his determination to become a free man.

For it positively [was] forbiden by law to teach a Negro to Wrote, So I had to fall back upon my own resources. Just as Frederick Douglass saw literacy as his ticket to freedom, so too does John Washington. With every written document having to pass through the hands of slave owners, it is no wonder that slaves developed their own secret means of communication—in slave spirituals for example, and perhaps in many other forms hidden from the historical record. Learning to read and write, the subject of Washington's next chapter, took considerable enterprise and determination on his part. In the postwar years, slaves would place reading and writing near the top of list of the most sought after fruits of liberty, alongside family reconstitution and land ownership.

4

Learning to Write

My Uncle George, Mothers Brother was one day in the lot Where I lived with Mr Ware and noticed me trying to copy the Writing Alphabet as shown in "Comleys Spelling Book," of that time, principally used by those trying to learn to read or Write. So he asked me what I was trying to do. I replied I am trying to Write, See here and seizing the pen, he wrote the following lines on a peice of Wallpaper,

"My Dear Mother,
I take this opportunity to write you a few lines to let you know that I am well,"

Now said he when you can do that much you you [sic] can write to your Mother. He was at best a poor writer, but the copy that he had just given me was as good as the best penmanship would have been because I could not get a Teacher of any kind or a Copy Book that I could understand. However I availed myself of the first chance I had to buy a 12 cent copy book, which was a most Wretched concern, and With its help I was most Successful in laying the foundation of a very bad Writer, for there Was nothing like form or Systom about the thing. About this time I, by some means or other, attracted the attention of the Rev Wm J. Walker, who was one day hanging paper in the house Where I lived.

Seeing my efforts at Writing he kindly Stoped, and wrote me a very good copy of the alphabet from which I soon learned to write Some kind of an inteligable hand and am Still trying to improve—But having never had a regular course of Spelling taught me, I am in consequence very defficent in every branch of a common and education.* So those who may be tempted to read this paper may possiably learn for the first time the disadvantages of of [sic] Slavery. With some of its attending evils.

COMMENT ON CHAPTER 4

I am in consequence very defficent in every branch of a common and education. Washington's handwriting, choice of words, and syntax are really quite remarkable, and he is being overly critical of himself.

Chapter 4

Learning to Write

My Uncle George _____ Nothing _____
___ Say in ___ lot ___ ___ _____
with ___ ___ and ___ ___ ___
_____ "The 10g7g Alphabet at ___
a "Complete Spelling Book" ___ ___
_____ _____ ___ by them ___
to ___ to _____ or write _____
__ ___ ___ ___ I was trying to do.
I ___ ___ I am trying to write ___
___ and _____ to ___ to ___ the
following ___ or a piece of wallpaper—

"My Dear Mother,

I take this opportunity
to write you a few lines to let you know
that I am well."

— I am also

and when you come to that much you
can ___ that much you can write
to your mother. ___ ___ was it best
___ ___ write __ ___ ___ the copy that
he had just given me did as good
as ___ ___ best penmanship could
_____ _____ because I could
not get a ___ of my own hand
to ___ copy but that I could
understand _____ I ___
myself of the first chance I had
to buy a 12 cent copy book which
was a ___ ___ _____ and
with its help I ___ just _____
in copying the foundation of a very
good writer, for ___ was nothing
like your ___ or written about
this _____ ___ this time

I am,
Your loving ___ & son,
___ ___ or ___
Mrs ___ J Walker, who was

5

Growing Up

SUNDAY SCHOOL. VISIT TO STAUNTON &C.

The Episcopal Church in Fredericksburg is Situated, on the North East corner of Princess Ann and George Street,* Surounded on the North, and East by the grave yard; Fronting on Princess Ann Street about Midway the Square Was a Small one Story brick In which I used to to [sic] go to a Sunday School Sundays afternoon and was taught the Cathacism and verses of the bible was read to us to get by heart.

I do not think much good resulted from this School, for we was not permitted to learn the A.B.C,s or to Spell, but Mrs Taliaferro was most zealous in sending Me to just Such places on Sundays as she would by this Means know where I was by asking Miss Olive Hanson, My Teacher, by the way she was a most kind and gentle Lady* and I often now think of her Sweet face and blue eyes, and feel a Spark of gratitude for the efforts on her part, for I really know She would have Learned me to read and wright if the Laws had permitted her so to do.

Notwithstanding Such Stringent rules as there was laid down for Me on Sundays I resorted to lieing and deception in order to get a few hours Play that was not allowed to me during the Week. Often I would steal some bodys boat and and [sic] with a lot of a bad boys as I could find go up or down the river for a row instead of going to to [sic] church where I was sent.

I had the greatest love for the river and boats, and Such risks as I passed through then for fun, I would not now undertake for any price. On Sunday in the early part of June or July 1852 I was ordered to church (in the afternoon, as usual) and instead of going, I met a party of Boys on My way to church, and we soon made an agreement to go across the River, and to "Coalters Fishing Shore"* which was a nice Secluded place for bathing. So we went and was Soon into the river in great glee.

But while we were all Some What afread that the Overseer, or Some one would drive us off—one of the Boys cried out here comes the Overseer!

All of us hastened out of the water to get our cloths and hide in the bushes to get them on. I unfortunately ran in Some vines of "Pison

Oaks," remained hid long enough to See there Was no one after us. When after playing amoung the [word scratched out] and rivelots [?] Wild flowers and Black berrys till near Sundown We went to our homes, Most of us with a lie in our Mouths, all passed off well until the latter part of the following week: When I broke out all over with "Pison Oak," Mrs Taliaferro nor any one in the house knew positively that it was the pison Oak as they had not the least idea that I had been near any such pison or even in the cuntry any where atal. But they Supposed I might have gotten hold of a peice in putting in wood a few days before.

Of course I told them I had not been in the Country any where. The Docter told Mrs Taliferro I had the humor in the Blood, and, after a due course of "Castor Oil," "Epsom Salts," etc etc advised that I be sent out in the country for a few weeks, in order to Save My Life. And as the Old Lady was awful afread of Sickness and the Doctors Bill, She concluded I Should be sent to Staunton, Virginia and allowed to Stay about 4 Weeks. I was delighted with the propositon and for fear She Should change he[r] Mind, I very conveinently began to get Sicker than ever.

But hearing her remark one day that she thought I was too Sick to travel, I made haste to be almost well the next day.*

In due time my cloths were made ready and packed in a letter valeze: with the following inscription on a Brass plate on the end: Redmon, U.S.N. that was the name of the former owner.

And in charge of Mr Phillips and his famely one night I bid fare well to my friends and was soon whirling over the R.F.P. Railroad on the way to Staunton, Va.

Arriving in Staunton the Second day after leaving home; the Meeting between Mother and Sisters and Brother was a most happy one. and long remembered.

I had traveled from Fredericksburg to Hanover Junction; by the "Richmond, Fredericksburg, and Potomac RailRoad," and thence to Woodville: by the "Virginia, *Central Rail Road," [footnote in original: *Now called the "Chesepeake & Ohio R.R"] where we took stages and continued the jurney across the Blue Ridge Mountin, arriving in Staunton about 11. o'clock P.M. on the Second Night from home.

I Remained in Staunton about 2 or 3 months, where I really enjoyed Myself Visiting the Mountins and Many other interesting places.

The "Deaf and Dumb Institution," "State Insane Asylum," "Virginia

Female Institute," and all combined to teach me the Same Sad lesson viz: the White Man's power and oppression of the Colored Slave.*

In October Mr Phillipps, one day, told me I would have to get ready and go back home to Fredericksburg, that week by the first opporteunity(!)

Now the opporteunity that they so much needed was, that Some White Person should take charge of my body and See to its Safe delivery in Fredericksburg. To be Sure they might write me a pass and put me in charge of a poor white Stage Driver, but he could only take me about 40 miles on my Jurney, Where I would have to be transferred to the cars: and in fact had to be transferred so often that there was a bare possibility that I might make my Escape and get to Some free State! Of course provided *I would do* such a disgraceful act:

However within a few days from the time I was notified a "white Man," one Dr Dowling, was duly charged with the responsibility of "Seeing me Safe home."*

We left Staunton one afternoon, after a sad and affecting parting with Mother and Sisters and Brother. My heart was full and my Voice choked with emotions and Mother and children wept, as only those do, who do not know that they may ever meet again on Earth. indeed either one might be Sold on the Auction Block next day. The Afternoon we left Staunton, about 2 or 3. O,clock was a chilly dull looking day, so frequent in the autumn, We crossed the "Blue Ridge,"* about dusk in a dense fog So thick that the horses attached to the Stage could not be Seen from the Windows. We Stopped at the little village of Cotville for the Night. That is, till 2. O clock A.M. When we got up and resumed our jurney to Woodville. And about 7. O clock that morning was Snugley seated in the Eastward bound train.

An Accident occured on the Train about 3 miles West of Charlottsville to one of the Colord Men employed on the train he was walking on a plank outside of the Mail Car.

The plank about 10 inches wide ran lenght way the car from one end to the other. So by holding on to an iron Rod above, one might pass to and fro without going through the mail car. this man whos name was Scott was passing to the front of the car when he steped upon an Orange peeling or Something or in passing by a fence that projected too near the cars he was dashed to the ground, Violently and his skull fractured. Some of the passengers Seeing the accident Informed the Conductor who had the Train backed and taken the man into the Car in which I was Seated (the Niggers Car) the blood flowed freely from the wounded man's head and ears until the Train arrived at Charlottesville where he was removed and Died afterwards I heard. Another Accident.

The Locomotive broke down just as we Stoped in at Charlottesville for breakfast. We were called in to breakfast but I could not eat any thing after seeing So much blood. Meantime A Hand Car had been Sent to the Next Station, Dinwiddie, for a Freight Locomotive awaiting there for our Train [to] pass. After we had been detained Several hours, and was just in the act of Starting on our Jurney again with the broken Engine repaired a little by the Engineer, The Freight Locomotive have in Sight [sic] and after Some disput between the Engineers in reference to who Should take the Train, Mostly Our first Engineer Claimed that Our Engine ("Blue Ridge") would probably draw us to Gordonsville quicker than the Old Freight Engine, to which that Engineer replyed if the Blue Ridge was allowed to Start with the Mail Train and Should break down he would not render any assistance, again:

So it was decided that the Freight Engineer and Locomotive, should take the Train to Gordonsville and Moseby, with the "Blue Ridge," should follow and take the Freight from Dinwiddie to Gordonsville.—

When our Train arrived at Dinwiddie We could see Nothing of the Crippled Locomotive behind us, but Just before we arrived at the next Station, we had a good view of the "Blue Ridge," and freight train coming at fine Speed after us until we reached Gordonsville much behind time, and too late to Stop for Dinner. The Hotel propritor Sent in to the Train by waiter enough of ham Sandwiches for all the passengers, Gratis.

We then Changed Engines for a beautiful one, the "Rock Fish." We left the "Blue Ridge" at Gordonsville and I never Seen it since.

The "Rock Fish," Made Splendid time to "Hanover Junction," where I changed cars For Fredericksburg there. Cars did not arrive at the Junction until about 8. Oclock P.M.

Consequently I had several hours to look around about the Junction.

There was nothing of interest worth noting here. — It was about 7 years before I Seen it again.

About 8. O'clock that night the Train From Richmond Stoped and I was soon Seated into a dark Car with a lot of county mail bags and

Boxes around me with no living Soul except myself. I was not doomed to Solitude long however: the Cars had been running but a Short time when one of the agents with a lantern in hand came into the car, Exclaimed hilow boy! what are you doing in here in the Dark: I told him I thought this was the Colord peoples car; Where is your Master I soon told him who I was traveling with, Well come along with me, said he, and led the way into another car which I found well lighted, comfortable, quite full of white passengers, mostly, asleep. I also soon fell asleep and was awake up in Fredericksburg.

The white people seemed very glad to see me* probabley being releived from anxiety of my possible escap to Freedom!

COMMENTS ON CHAPTER 5

The Episcopal Church in Fredericksburg is Situated, on the North East corner of Princess Ann and George Street. St. George's Episcopal Church is the oldest church in Fredericksburg, first built in 1732. George Washington and his mother worshiped here, as well as Washington's sister Betty Fielding and other relatives. Revolutionary War generals Hugh Mercer and George Weedon were also members, as was William Paul, brother of John Paul Jones. In 1815, under the leadership of the Reverend Edward McGuire, who served as rector from 1813 until 1857, the wooden building was replaced by a brick structure, to which Washington refers. In 1849 the present Romanesque revival–style structure replaced the brick building. In the 1850s, a town clock was installed in the tower of the church. During the 1862 battle of Fredericksburg, the church was hit by shellfire at least twenty-five times, and the four-piece communion set was stolen. It was not returned complete for seventy years. In Washington's time, box pews were sold to families who paid annual rents for the building and the operation of the church. Some worshipers important to the history of this period include J. B. Ficklin, a wealthy flour miller who became a Unionist during the Civil War and paid a rental fee of $450 for pew 3; M. Slaughter, thé wartime mayor, who was charged $325 for pew 10; Duff Green, who attempted to prevent Ficklin from collecting war damages after the war by testifying falsely that he was a Confederate sympathizer, who paid $225 for pew 83; and T. B. Barton, the commonwealth's attorney, who surrendered the town to federal authorities before the battle of Fredericksburg. He paid $405 for pew 100.[1]

By the way she was a most kind and gentle Lady. Here is an example of how Washington addressed and treated whites for whom he had great respect. Not surprisingly, he favored those whites who treated him kindly and those who tried in some way to help compensate for slavery's disadvantages, despite society's discouragement of interracial exchanges in custom and law.

We soon made an agreement to go across the River, and to "Coalters Fishing Shore." Coalters Fishing Shore is one of those "coordinates of freedom" that Washington placed on his map of the area (see appendix).

But hearing her remark one day that she thought I was too Sick to travel, I made haste to be almost well the next day. The psychological impact of slavery has taken many interpretive twists and turns. One historian has argued that slavery made "Sambos" out of its victims in a process of infantilization. Stuttering, downcast looks, and excessive mannerliness have all been interpreted as signs of psychological scarring. Others have pointed to numerous acts of resistance and a few well-known slave rebellions to argue that slaves, rather than being passive victims, found the means to resist infantilization. No doubt slaves reacted in both ways. These incidents described by Washington give ample evidence of small daily acts of defiance, as he uses lies and dissimulation to achieve his ends. His later behavior reveals no hesitation in challenging slavery or reluctance to do whatever is necessary to gain freedom.[2] Mostly, his resistance is expressed in the form of small, spontaneous, and individual challenges to enslavement, rather than in any organized collective way. Nevertheless, when the moment presented itself, as it did with the advance of the Union forces, Washington did not hesitate to emancipate himself.

All combined to teach me the Same Sad lesson viz: the White Man's power and oppression of the Colored Slave. Washington's observation here is very interesting. The institutions he mentions were segregated but composed of members of both races. Does he mean that the majority of inmates he saw were black? Clearly he sees the institutions as instruments of power and control, rather than the nineteenth century's social experiment in behavioral modification and rehabilitation, as envisioned by altruistic social reformers of the age.[3]

I was notified a "white Man," one Dr Dowling, was duly charged with the responsibility of "Seeing me Safe home." Despite their claims that their slaves were contented, slaveholders were reluctant to let them out of sight. Yet it was difficult to escape and get to a free state of the North, and even if a slave got away, there was no certainty of freedom in the North.

We crossed the "Blue Ridge." Washington here recalls his journey along the Rockfish Gap Turnpike, a 43½-mile dirt toll road opened in 1826. Also known as the Staunton and James River Turnpike, the road began in Staunton in the Shenandoah Valley and went east to Waynesboro, through Rockfish Gap in the Blue Ridge Mountains and Israel's Gap in the smaller Ragged Mountains. It terminated in Scottsville on the James River. The turnpike was nearly impassable at low points between the Blue Ridge and Ragged Mountains after periods of heavy rains.[4] Scottsville, which Washington probably meant by "Cotville," was not on any rail line at the time, and he probably had to travel west to "Woodville" to pick up the Orange and Alexandria Railroad that connected Lynchburg and Alexandria via Charlottesville.

The white people seemed very glad to see me. Washington has no delusions that the whites of Fredericksburg welcome him back because of any affection for him. Rather, he attributes their expressions of welcome to their anxiety over slaves escaping.

6

Finding a Wife

The years of 1853–54 was passed in the usual routine of Slave life with its Many Sorrows and fears and fiting hopes of Escape to Freedom. So far as I was concerned I was kept unusually close,* never permitted to pass the limits of the lot after Sundown without a permission and limited time to return which must be punctually obeyed if I had any desire to go out again in a reasonable time.

On Sundays the Same of "Rules" mentioned in Chapter 5 was Strictly Enforced which if disobeyed at any one time would be Sufficent cause to keep me in many Sundays thereafter. Imagine a boy about 16 or 17 years of age in good health with many rolicking fun loving companions playing in full Sight of the house, on a bright Sunday Morning in the Months of May or June, with a beautiful Surrounding Country spread out for miles around visible to the naked Eye; With the Sweet Scent of Clover, Locust Blossoms, Hunnysuckle, Apple, Cherry, and various Fruit Trees almost Ripened, and all nature Clothed with beauty, that can not be describe—And that boy only permitted to See all this from an open window.*

Not permitted to go out and See and Smell the Work of Him, who created all things.

Imagine Such a case, I say, and you will have a very faint glimmer of my case at that time.

I was very Seldom allowed to visit any partys of young company except Fairs which was held for the benefit of one of the Colored Churches as there was not but Two The "African Baptist," and "Little Wesley" Methodist. Some time a fair would be opened at a private house for the benefit of some poor person trying to make up money to finish paying for them selves or otherwise afflicted.

But nothing of the kind could be had without a permitt from the Mayor of the Town. Such specifying the times the fair should be closed, which had to be Strictly adhered to. All Such "Fairs" had to be held During the "Easter," "Whitsentide" or "Christmas Hollidays."

To these fairs some times I was permitted to go which to me was almost a heavenly boon.

It was at one of these fairs I frequently met Miss Annie E. Gordon, having received an Introduction through a friend in a rather Singular manner.

It was as follows, I had wrote a Valentine a few months previous for a friend of mine. Austin Bunday who had it Directed to this young Lady.

I then obtained a promise from him that I would accompany him to his next visit to this Lady and be introduced under the assumed name of Mr John Bunday his Brother. This plan was duly carried out and Miss Annie Gordon was fully Satisfied that it was My true name—Until the Hollidays of "Easter," or Whitsentide 1853. When by an accedent, She over heard Some other Young Ladies of my acquaintance Call me by my right Name. when she asked me what it Meant, and I then told her of the fact: She Seemed Some what annoyed, but it was alright in the course of time. I had conceived a particular fancy for this Young girl at first Sight.*

I was then very bashful and backward in Speech. With probably no kind of idea of love making. Only this girl had a Sad, but very pretty face, and Shy half Scared look as if she thought I would bite her. She talked but little in My presence and then So low you might have thought she was talking to herself. So I some time visited her at her Mothers or saw her at the Churches and in the Street. I did not visit her often for a long time afterward.

The African Baptist Church was situated on the N.E. cor. of Sophia and Hanover Sts (At the time I am Speaking of the "White people," worshiped in the upper part of the Building and the "Colord people," in the Basement.) In the Spring of 1855, A great Revival of Religion prevailed among both White and Colord people of that church and a great many was added to its membership.

Amoung these that joined at that time was many young Men and Young Women of my particular friends.

It was during this revival that I was Sincerly trubbled about the Salvation of my Soul. And about the 25th of May I was converted and found the Saviour precious to my Soul, and heavenly Joyes Manefested, and began to be felt at that time, are Still like burning coals; fanned by the breeze (after a lapse of Nearly 17 years) and is to this day the most precious assurance of My life, God grant me more faith and a better understanding, for these things let rocks and hills their lasting Silance breake; And all harmonious human Tounges their Saviours praises Speak. I was Baptised in the Rappahannock River at Fredericksburg, Va. by Rev. Wm F. Broaddus June 13th 1856.

And many happy moments have I spent with the Church in its Joys and Sorrows at that place.* I was permitted to attend divine Service on Sundays but at nights I was not allowed to go out but little—During my close imprisonment (I do not know what else to call it) The "Word of God," was to me a Source of Unfailing pleasure. I became a close reader of the Bible. And wrote many comments on different Chapters which has since been lost.

It was during the autumn of 1856, that I Experienced my first attack of Sickness of any duration, Which soon developed itself into a Severe and protracted case of Typhoid Fever which wore itself off in "Chills and Fevers," about 3 months from the commencement.

Be it Said to their credit that Mrs. Taliaferro and her son Wm Ware was the most attentive to me during my whole sickness.* I could not have been better attended to by my nearest Relations.

I have often since Wished it had pleased "Devine Providence," to have taken me from this world of Sin then*—When I had not, as Now Seen so Much of the Exceeding "Sinfullness of Sin."

I Remained on the lot in service with Mr Ware and his mother, until Jaunary 1st 1869.* When I was hired to Wm T. Heart, next door, Where I had to Drive Horses, Attend a cow, help in the Garden and everything else like work. But to me the change was very agreeable indeed all Sunday and night restrictions was removed except what was really nessesary. My Clothing was abundant and good. My opporteunities to make money for Myself was increased tenfold. I lived with Mrs Hart one year 1859.—

January 1st 1860 I went to live with Messrs Alexander & Gibbs, tobbacco Manufactorers, where I, in a month or Two learned the art of preparing Tobacco for the Mill.*

We were all "Tasked," to Twist from 66 1/8 to 100 lbs per day. All the Work we could do over the task we got paid for which was *our own money*, not our Masters in this way some of us could make $3.00 or 4 extra in a week.*

The Factory weeks began on Saturdays and ended on Fridays, When the Books were posted and all the men that had over work were paid promply on Saturday.

But if any one failed to have completed his Task the Book would be generally resorted to—In a Tobacco Factory, the "Twisters," generally have one or Two boys, sometimes Women, for Stemming the Tobacco to be "Twisted"*; The Factorys is kept very clean, and Warmed in Winter. from early Morning till late at Night could be heard The Noise of the Macheinry and Singing of the hands in one incessant din. in a Tobacco Factory Some of the finest Singing known to the Colord Race could frequently be heard*—I was only permmitted to live one year in consequence of the Threatning position of the Southern States. the firm of Alexander & Gibbs suspended operation. this year in the Factory was to me more like "Freedom," than any I had known Since I was a very small boy. We began Work at 7. O clock in the Morning Stoped from 1. to 2. o,clock for dinner—Stopped Work at 6 P.M. If we chose to make Extra work We began at any hour Before 7. and Worked Some time till 9. P.M. the Sesession of South Carolina, and the threatened close of business between the North and South, caused the Suspension of work in this factory early in December 1860.

COMMENTS ON CHAPTER 6

So far as I was concerned I was kept unusually close. North-South tensions were increasing during this period. The Compromise of 1850 included a new Fugitive Slave Act, a pro-southern provision that once again attempted to appease the South with reassurances that the North would help southern slave owners capture their runaway slaves. Instead of lessening North-South tensions, it exacerbated them because many northerners refused to be drawn into the distasteful business of helping southerners seize slave runaways.

That boy only permitted to See all this from an open window. Washington points to the sensory markers of freedom and the gift of unrestricted movement, pleasures that few would understand and appreciate except those who arose each day to face the harsh realities of another day in slavery.

I had conceived a particular fancy for this Young girl at first Sight. Very rarely do scholars get to witness courtship among slaves because few of these narratives exist—in fact none of which I am aware that treat the romantic lives of the slaves. There is no indication whether Austin Bunday, who assisted in the tryst, is another slave, a free black, or a white friend. Showing great respect, Washington gives Annie's full name. The awkward shyness of two suitors meeting, each more enchanted than they want to reveal, seems very natural.

And many happy moments have I spent with the Church in its Joys and Sorrows at that place. This is the same church formerly owned by whites but sold to become the African Baptist Church in 1854. Apparently, a number of white parishioners continued to attend. Washington's conversion experience is still vivid in his mind over a decade and a half later. Another unanticipated circumstance is his baptism by a white minister. Rev. William Broaddus, politically a Whig, was on the town council that surrendered the town to the Union forces in April. In August 1862, Broaddus was imprisoned for six weeks in the Old Capitol prison along with eighteen other Fredericksburgers.[1] There is also great irony here. The same river that carried slaves to Fredericksburg immersed them in baptism, and later carried them to freedom.

Be it Said to their credit that Mrs. Taliaferro and her son Wm Ware was the most attentive to me during my whole sickness. Although Washington does not question their intentions, his owners' concern for his welfare cannot be divorced from their fear of losing a valuable property. The attentiveness of the owner and her son to Washington's illness could also be explained in terms of his special status as a household slave and maybe as a family member.

I have often since Wished it had pleased "Devine Providence," to have taken me from this world of Sin then. Washington's religious sensibilities may be surprising in light of the disdain he had shown for worship at the behest of Catherine Taliaferro, but the fact that Washington had joined the Fredericksburg Baptist Church may indicate the appeal of evangelical Christianity among those growing up in slavery. In other Baptist churches in antebellum Virginia, slaves were eager to maintain their membership in the community, even if they did not receive the gospel as preached by white ministers.[2] As has been witnessed throughout the history of Christianity, conversions are often unexpected and yet profoundly transformative, and Washington's awakening to the sinfulness of the world reflects Baptist theological sensibilities.

I Remained on the lot in service with Mr Ware and his mother, until January 1st 1869. Washington clearly writes "1869" in the text. He means 1859, however.

I went to live with Messrs Alexander & Gibbs, tobbacco Manufactorers, where I, in a month or Two learned the art of preparing Tobacco for the Mill. Hiring out of slaves was a source of income for slave owners, and tobacco manufacturers paid some of the highest wages to owners of any antebellum industry. Beyond their time at work, tobacco manufacturers did not exercise any disciplinary or supervisory authority over enslaved workers. The skills Washington was learning in the tobacco industry could make him much more valuable, though William Ware would have been unaware of this.

The Fredericksburg tobacco factory was a three-story brick building located on the north side of Prussia Street and just west of Princess Anne Street. As recorded by Noel Harrison, in 1860 the factory had 50 operatives and employed steam power and manual labor to produce 1,000 pounds of "leaf, lug, smoking & manufactured tobacco" each day. Additives to the tobacco produced such alluring and intriguing names as "Oriental Orange Bloom," "Medicated Anti-Nervous," "Single Star," "Honey Cherry," and "Solferino." The proprietors hired thirteen slaves: a 35-year-old black male and a 34-year-old black male, both owned by J. G. Beverley; a 50-year-old black male owned by "Moncure"; a 35-year-old black male owned by a Colonel Wright; a 50-year-old black male owned by E. H. Henry; a 45-year-old black male, an 18-year-old mulatto male, an 11-year-old mulatto male, and a 10-year-old black male, all owned by James Lacy; a 20-year-old black male owned by the estate of R. W. Downer; a 50-year-old black male owned by M. R. Garnett; and a 45-year-old black female and a 9-year-old black male, both owned by Joseph Trigg. During the war the factory became a hospital for both Union and Confederate soldiers.[3]

Some of us could make $3.00 or 4 extra in a week. Washington provides rare insight into slave work in a factory setting, how tobacco was processed, how hired-out slaves felt about industrial labor, and the economic opportunity such labor offered to make extra money that slaves could use to purchase their freedom or the freedom of loved ones. British visitor Alexander Mackay witnessed one enslaved Richmond tobacco worker striving to earn extra pay. Mackay found out that the man sometimes earned as much as ten dollars a week for exceeding his task work and had already earned enough to purchase his wife's freedom. He was working hard to buy his own freedom.[4]

In 1860, there were 261 tobacco factories in Virginia, employing 11,382 workers. Tobacco factories got slaves through purchase or hire. Hiring was on the increase in the 1850s: In 1850, 42 percent of slaves were hired; in 1860, 52 percent were hired. Hiring was popular because it required no large outlay of cash. Farmers and planters who found themselves with too many slaves could hire out their surplus labor, with prices averaging 12 to 15 percent of a slave's value. Some used the practice to rid themselves of troublemakers. In 1833, factory hands were hired for $60 to $70 a year. By 1860, the rate was as high as $225 for experienced hand labor in Petersburg, but the average remained at $100 to $200 for trained adults.[5]

Besides compensation for overtime, manufacturers also gave money to slaves for food and lodging. Giving slaves freedom to find their own food and shelter loosened the reins of bondage. Hires enjoyed quasi-freedom at night, yet in Richmond, at least, they created serious difficulties as they roamed the city looking for places to stay. They found lodging wherever they could, in private rooms, with wives who were employed in the city as domestic slaves. For many who worked in Richmond factories, however, home was an alley, a warehouse, a stable, or a shed. In some cases board money covered meals; other slaves got food by stealing or bribing cooks. As increased freedom created problems of control, local authorities made attempts to set rules on boarding out, but these were fruitless. The city absorbed into its rooming houses, kitchens, and alleyways thousands of slave hires each night, who settled in among the large free black population, far away from the eyes of a slaveholder, factory owner, or overseer. Many ran away, but most became customers of free people of African descent who cooked, cleaned, and kept house for them.[6]

Beyond wages to masters of about $120–$125 per year by the late 1850s for an adult male tobacco worker, and boarding-out money and the extra wages paid to slaves, factory owners were responsible for slaves' clothing.[7] Tobacco manufacturers often provided clothing bought in bulk from local merchants, usually course osnaburgs, cottonades, heavy yarn socks, rough blankets, and brogans—all very similar to other slave clothing. Some slaves stole to get clothes, especially coats and shoes. As for medical care, no formal arrangement existed. Some manufacturers hired physicians; others ignored health needs.

In a Tobacco Factory, the "Twisters," generally have one or Two boys, sometimes Women, for Stemming the Tobacco to be "Twisted." Tobacco work involved a series of tasks that required dexterity and strength. Four steps were necessary in the manufacture of chewing tobacco, the most common tobacco product: stemming, flavoring, lumpmaking, and prizing. Stemming involved moistening the leaves to make them pliable, then stripping out the central veins. Flavoring required dipping tobacco leaves into a syrupy mixture of licorice and sugar and cooking them in big kettles. Then workers placed the leaves in the open air to dry and sprinkled a mixture of rum, sweet oil, and spices on them to make them aromatic. Boys and women accomplished these steps. In lumpmaking, workers molded the leaves into rectangular plugs and wrapped them in unflavored leaves of high quality. If twists were desired instead of plugs, the leaves were given to twisters rather than lumpmakers, who wove the leaves into a figure-eight form. Twisting or lumpmaking required nimbleness and dexterity, so it was a job performed frequently by young boys. Prizing involved placing the lumps on divided wooden patterned presses and forcing the plugs into their proper shape and firmness.[8] It had to be done several times to align the edges perfectly for packing. Prizing was the most strenuous job in the factory, and prizemen were chosen for their strength. It would take six to eight men to pull the lever that turned the screw on the press, and with each pull "they uttered a simultaneous noise in their throats, a sort of half cough, and half bark."[9] Slaves worked stripped to the waist in the prizing room, heaving at the long iron arms that turned the screws. Prizing could be mechanized, but with slave labor there was no incentive for that capital investment.

In a Tobacco Factory Some of the finest Singing known to the Colord Race could frequently be heard. Singing at work was a custom that became popular to relieve the monotony and harshness of the tasks. Spirituals were popular work songs. Twisters carried out their tasks in a seesaw motion, while singing together in harmony a hymn or sometimes "an impromptu chant" that at a distance sounded plaintive. William Cullen Bryant described slaves singing in a factory this way: "As we entered the room we heard a murmur of psalmody running through the sable assembly, which now and then swelled into a strain of very tolerable music." Sometimes the workers sang all day long; other times not a note. It was done spontaneously. Some factory owners limited singing or permitted it only at certain times.[10]

7

The War Comes

January 1st 1861. I was Sent to Richmond, Va to be hired out. I had long desired to go to Richmond. I had been told by My friends it was a good Place to make money for Myself and I wanted to go there.

So with a great many of old Friends, I was placed in the Care of Mr Hay Hoomes, hireing agent, and (on the Cars) Started to Richmond where We arrived about 3. O,clock the Same day. And I was hired to one Zetelle, an Eating Saloon keeper. there was no Liquors kept there.*

I lived with him six months When he Sold the place to a man named Wendlinger. both of these Men Were low, mean and course. they treated their Servants cruelly after Whipping them their selves or Sending them to the Slave jail to be whipped,* Where it was done fearfully for 50 cents.

I got along unusally well with both men, Especially the latter.

I was living there when the Southern Slave holders in open Rebellion fired on Fort Sumter. little did they then think that they were Firing the Death-knell of Slavery, and little did I think that my deliverence was So near at hand. The fireing on Fort Sumter occured April 12, 1861, and from that time forward Richmond became the seat of the Rebellion. Thousands of Troops was Sent to Richmond from all parts of the South on their way to Washington, as They Said. and So many troops of all discription was landed there that it appeared to be an impossiability, to us, Colord people; that they could ever be conquord.

In July 1861. the 21st day the Union Army, and the Rebels met at Bulls Run and a great Battle was fought and the Union army was defeated. Already the Slaves had been Escaping into the Union armys lines* and Many thereby getting of[f] to the Free States. I could read the papers and eagerly Watched them for tidings of the War Which had began in earnest. almost every day brought news of Battles. The Union troops was called "Yankees and the Southern "Rebs." It had now become a well known fact that Slaves was daily Making their escape into the Union lines. So at Christmas 1861, I left Richmond, having been provided with a pass and fare to Fredericksburg Va.

I told Mr Wendlinger and my fellow Servants good by They expected me back the 1st of Janaury again to live with them another year.

Soon after I arrived in Fredericksburg I Sought and obtained a home for the Year of 1862, at the "Shakespear House," part of the time as "Steward," and the balance as Bar-keeper—My Master was not pleased when he heard of my intention to remain in Fredericksburg that year; he Seemed to think I wanted to remain too near the "Yankees," though he did not tell me these words.

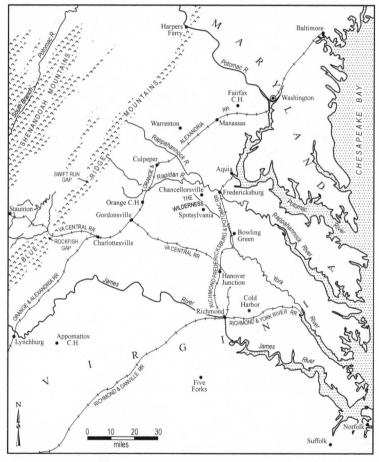

Map of Virginia during the Civil War, adapted from *Atlas of American History* (New York: Scribner's, 1984), 162. Original drawn under supervision of Douglas Southall Freeman. Redrawn by Mary Lee Eggart.

View of Fredericksburg from east bank of Rappahannock River, 1862–63. From Library of Congress, Prints and Photographs Division.

The War Was getting hoter Every day, and the Yankees had approched Within a few Miles of the Town more than once.* The later part of Febraury, 1862, the Rebs began to withdraw their forces from the Aquia Creek Landing which Was then the terminus of the "Richmond Fredericksburg and Potomac Railroad." Early in March the Rebs began to fall back from the Potomack River.

The Town was now filled with Rebel Soilders, and their Outrages and dastardly acts toward the colord people can not be told. It became dangerous to be out atal of nights. The Whites Was hastening their Slaves off to Safer places of refuge.

A great many Slave Men were Sent into the Rebel army as Drivers, Cooks, Hostlers and any thing Else they could do.*

The Firm of Payton & Mazine who hired me were both Officers in the Rebel Army.* the first Captain in the 30th Regiment of Virginia; the later was a Lieutanant in the Same Regiment, was at home, on the Sick list, and in charge of the Hotel.

About the Last of March there was a good deal of talk about Evacuateing Fredericksburg.* Which was Soon after Commenced. by the 15th of April Most of the Troops had been Withdrawn. On the night of the 15th or 16th the Yankees advanced and had a Skirmish, and drove in the Rebel picketts with Some of them Wounded and the others Most frightfully Scared.

The Propietors of the Shakespear now told Me the house would have to be closed very Soon in consequence of the near approach of the Yankees; and that I would have to go to Saulsbury, North Carolina. to Wait on Capt Payton the balance of the Year.

I could not very well Make any objection as the Firm had always treated Me Well and paid Me besides, for attending the Bar for them, When I was hired only for a Dining room Servant. I was easily induced to change from the Dining room for $37.00 and Extra Money every Week.

So When I was told that I would have to go to Saulsbery I became greatly alarmed* and began to fear that the object in Sending me down there, Was to be done to get me out of the reach of the Yankees.

and I Secretly resolved not to go

But I made them beleive I was Most anxious to go.

In fact I made them beleive I was terebelely afred of the Yankees, any Way.

My Master was well satisfied at My appearant disposition, and told Me I was quite Right, for if the Yankees were to catch me they would Send me to Cuba or cut my hands off or otherwise Maltreat Me.* I of course pretended to beleive all they said but knew they were lieing all the while. As Soon as they told me When I had to Start, I Intended to conceale Myself and Wait the approach of the Yankees and When once in the lines I intended to go to Detroit, Michigan Where I had an Uncle living.

COMMENTS ON CHAPTER 7

I was hired to one Zetelle, an Eating Saloon keeper. there was no Liquors kept there. Eating saloons varied in the practice of serving liquor. The Shakespeare Hotel in Fredericksburg, where Washington was working when the Union forces advanced on the town, did serve liquor. The hotel was a three-story brick structure located on the east side of Caroline Street between George and Hanover streets. In 1860 the proprietor advertised that the hotel had been converted to the "European plan" with rooms without regular meals, the guests able to order at their leisure. He promised a larder "plentifully supplied with the best fare the markets afford . . . [including] WILD FOWL, FISH, OYSTERS, &c. The BAR will be found to contain every variety and excellence of LIQUORS and CIGARS." A billiard room was also attached to the hotel. In 1864, a Union chaplain who stayed at the hotel gave more definition to the European plan. In disgust, he reported "four noted whores from Washington" as house guests and claimed the proprietors were keeping a house of prostitution. He called Mr. Hunt, one of the proprietors, a "gambler & swindler" and Mr. Young, the former mayor, a "low whore house pimp [who] instead [of] serving his country . . . is living off the earnings of lude [sic] women."[1]

Prostitution did flourish in Fredericksburg during the Civil War as Union and Confederate soldiers found relief from the boredom of garrison duty. In June 1862, a Fredericksburg newspaper reported that the Union provost guard had arrested a Pennsylvania artilleryman in "female dress and very disorderly" in the vicinity of the Shakespeare, "then in its bawdy heyday." The next month, the ever-vigilant Union general Marsena Patrick found the town "full of brothels" and immediately set about dispersing members of "the loose population." But the loose population soon found another clientele in Confederate counterparts, eager customers from Fredericksburg's Confederate garrison. In April 1863, a Confederate soldier found it necessary to write in a letter to his wife that he did not "lust after the base women of this town of which there is a number."[2]

Sending them to the Slave jail to be whipped. Whipping jails were not uncommon; they were used by owners to punish slave troublemakers. Captain Pickett, a constable in Falmouth, made his living whipping slaves. Young white boys would scramble for positions at the windows to watch the whippings. Moncure Conway spent some time at Pickett's "small prison-like building" and watched with "a mixture of curiosity and revulsion." Later Conway wrote: "A glimpse I once had of the old man with lash lifted over the tender form of a young girl, abided in my memory." In the 1850s Captain Pickett hanged himself.[3]

Already the Slaves had been Escaping into the Union armys lines. Washington's knowledge of the events of the Civil War is remarkable, belying any notion that slaves did not know about what was going on in this war. His reference to slaves fleeing to Union lines is an example. In May 1861, General Benjamin Butler—"Beast Butler" as many pro-southerners called him—of the Union army was in command of troops at Fortress Monroe near Norfolk, Virginia. Three slaves who had been working on Confederate fortifications escaped to Butler's lines. He refused to return them and labeled them "contraband of war." The phrase caught on, and for the rest of the war, slaves who entered Union lines were known as "contrabands." Word circulated among slaves in the Virginia peninsula, and by August one thousand contrabands were in Butler's camps. Abolitionists began to make plans to establish schools and send missionary teachers to the camps of contrabands. Before the war ended, thousands trailed the Union troops, and many former slave men enlisted in the Union army and served in black regiments known collectively as the United States Colored Troops.[4]

The Yankees had approched Within a few Miles of the Town more than once. Although Washington describes troop movements in and out of the Fredericksburg area, the real battle for Fredericksburg did not take place until 13 December 1862, after his narrative closes.[5]

A great many Slave Men were Sent into the Rebel army as Drivers, Cooks, Hostlers and any thing Else they could do. The Confederate command refused to enlist slaves in the military, a mistake that cost them in two ways: exacerbation of an already short supply of Confederate manpower to wage the war and the attrition of slave men who fled to fight in the Union armies, not only making them unavailable for menial labor but also potentially providing the North with additional soldiers. From the Confederates' point of view, however, making slaves serve effectively as Confederate soldiers must have seemed unlikely.

The Firm of Payton & Mazine who hired me were both Officers in the Rebel Army. Washington's memory was precise. James Mazeen had been elected a lieutenant in Company A of the Thirtieth Virginia Infantry in January 1862 but because of illness did not take that post until 22

April, shortly after Fredericksburg fell temporarily to Union forces. The 47-year-old grocer and manager of the Shakespeare Hotel resigned from the Thirtieth Virginia on 22 October after six months' service. The husband of Mary Mazeen and father of James R. and William Mazeen—who would have been teenagers when their father saw Confederate service— survived the war and died in 1875 at age sixty-two. He probably owned no slaves before the war. Afterwards he ran a Fredericksburg restaurant and took care of his elderly mother Mary while his son James tended the bar. Mazeen's partner was George H. Peyton, who entered service as a lieutenant in Company A of the Thirtieth Virginia. Peyton was a 32-year-old restaurant proprietor when he hired Washington from his owner. Like Mazeen, Peyton enlisted in the Thirtieth Virginia on 22 April, and he was elected captain later that summer, on 15 July. The 1860 census taker recorded that Peyton owned real estate valued at $2,000 and $6,000 in personal property, which included several slaves, some of whom he owned jointly or hired out to clients. In June 1860, Peyton and his wife Lucy lived in Fredericksburg with seven children, five boys and two girls, aged nine months to thirteen years.[6] Peyton also survived the war and apparently died on 4 September 1883 at age fifty-five.

If Peyton lamented the Union army taking Fredericksburg in April, he probably rejoiced as he and the men of the Thirtieth Virginia watched their fellow Confederates destroy the cream of General Ambrose E. Burnside's Army of the Potomac in the battle of Fredericksburg that December. They surveyed the carnage from an elevated vantage point on 11 December. Being familiar with the terrain, the Thirtieth was assigned to capture supplies abandoned by the Union army in their defeat and confusion. As men in the hospitality business, however, Peyton and Mazeen were probably disgusted by the rations they received after the battle, in a nearby winter camp. One soldier from neighboring Caroline County complained the beef was so revolting that "I sometimes think they kill men to keep them from dying" from the food. Poor provisions may have sickened Peyton, or his illness may have been brought on by exposure during one of the massive snowball fights men in camp enjoyed during their winter of 1862–63; whatever the cause, he was dropped from the regiment in February and allowed to resign in March 1863. Peyton was fortunate to survive; disease killed two men on both sides during the Civil War for every one killed in battle.[7]

There was a good deal of talk about Evacuateing Fredericksburg. The news quickly reached Richmond of the Union advances on Fredericksburg. In anticipation of its fall, the telegraph equipment and railroad cars were removed so that the Union could not use the city's communications and transportation infrastructure. The *Richmond Daily Dispatch* reported that on 16 April the Union forces "threw a few shells across the river, but there being no response, the firing soon ceased." The fleeing Confederates destroyed whatever they thought valuable to the advancing forces. According to the *Dispatch,* "three steamers, the St. Nicholas, the Virginia, and the Eureka, and some thirty sail vessels, lying at the wharf, loaded with grain, with a considerable quantity of cotton piled near the depot, were set on fire by our men and destroyed. The troops that were in and near the place, very few in number, and utterly inadequate to make a defense against a considerable force, evacuated Fredericksburg after having performed the duties required of them." The newspaper noted that "many of the citizens also left, abandoning their property to the 'tender mercies' of the enemy." The report mentions the skirmish Washington recalls here: "On the night previous some small skirmish as took place above Falmouth, in which the enemy was repulsed; but our men afterwards fell back. Mr. Charles Ticket, of Stafford, was taken prisoner, and we hear that one or two were killed. A wounded Yankee was captured by our pickets and sent down by the train yesterday morning, but he died before reaching Ashland. This man stated that the Federal force amounted to six thousand, and that they approached Fredericksburg from Fauquier county."[8] Approaching from the north, so as to "cover" Washington, D.C., the Union army threatened Fredericksburg, though the Richmond paper expressed doubt that the "Yankees" would or could go very far south of Fredericksburg without serious resistance.

When I was told that I would have to go to Saulsbery I became greatly alarmed. Washington mentions Saulsbury (Salisbury), North Carolina, earlier in the chapter.

If the Yankees were to catch me they would Send me to Cuba or cut my hands off or otherwise Maltreat Me. It was common for masters, especially in areas close to the front lines, to try to frighten slaves into loyalty by spreading rumors about how horribly the Yankees treated captured slaves. Many slaves did believe that Union soldiers were "devils" come to devour them and their children. Yet many other slaves routinely pretended to believe what whites told them, an attitude historians have labeled "wearing masks." It is evident from Washington's experience that some enslaved people had their own idea of what the arrival of the Union army meant for them. Ironically, it was southern whites' accusations against northerners that gave many slaves the sense that the U.S. Army was a beacon of liberty for them before U.S. officials decided to use the threat of emancipation as a war measure. Before secession, slaveholders and southern partisans had yelled themselves hoarse about the supposed abolitionism rampant among Yankees, Republicans, and southerners under their influence. In doing so, they unintentionally convinced many slaves that any Union army would in fact be an abolitionist army. Although southern partisans insisted the opposite and tried to demonize northerners when threatened, they had already laid the groundwork for slaves to view "Father Abraham" and his army as ushering in a time of Jubilee when slaves would be released from their bondage.

When Washington encountered the Army of the Potomac in 1862, President Abraham Lincoln had neither promised nor even seriously considered an emancipation proclamation. In fact, he countermanded generals' field orders granting liberty to runaway slaves and refused to allow black troops to enlist in combat units, insisting the Civil War was a white man's fight for political union. Washington shows an acute sensibility for understanding how local occurrences fit into the broader canvas of events, knowing before Lincoln did that the army's presence portended the end of slavery.

8

First Night of Freedom

April 18th 1862, Was "Good-Friday,"* the Day was a mild pleasant one with the Sun shining brightly and every thing unusally quite [sic]. the Hotel was crowded with boarders who was Seated at breakfast a rumor had been circulated amoung them that the Yankees Was advancing, but nobody Seemed to beleive it, until Every body Was Startled by Several reports of cannon.

Then in an instant all Was Wild confusion as a calvary Man dashed into the Dining Room and Said "The Yankees is in Falmouth." Every body was on their feet at once, No-body finished but Some ran to their rooms to get a few things, Officers and Soilders hurried to their Quarters Every Where Was hurried Words and hasty foot Steps.

Mr Mazene Who had hurried to his room now came running back called me out in the Hall and thrust a roll of Bank notes in my hand and hurriedly told me to pay off all the Servants, and Shut up the house and take charge of every thing. "If the Yankees catch Me they will kill me So I can't Stay here,["] "Said he" and was off at full speed like the Wind. In less time than it takes me to Write these lines, every White Man was out the house. Every Man Servant was out on the house top looking over the River at the Yankees for their glistening bayonets could easiely be Seen I could not begin to Express My New born hopes for I felt already like I was certain of my freedom now.

By this time the Two Bridges crossing the River here was on fire the Match having been applied by the retreating rebels. 18 vessels and 2 steamers at the Wharf was also burning.

In 2 hours from the firing of the First gun, Every Store in town was closed. Every White Man had run away or hid himself Every White Woman had Shut themselves in doors. No one could be seen on the Streets but the Colord people. and every one of them Seemed to be in the best of humor. Every rebel Soilder had left the town and only a few of them hid in the Woods West of the town Watching. The Yankees turned out to be the 1st Brigade of "Kings Division,"* of McDowells Corpse [sic], under Brigader Genl Auger, having advanced as far as

Falmouth they had stoped on Ficklins, Hill over looking the little town. Genl Auger discovered a rebel Artillery on the oppisite Side of the river, Who after Setting fire to the Bridge was fireing at the Piers trying to knock them down the "Yankees" Soon turned Several Peices loose on the rebels who after a few Shots beat a hasty retreat; coming through Fredericksburg a a [sic] break neck speed as if the "Yankees" was at their heels.

Instead of across the river Without a Ford, and all the Bridges burnt.

As Soon as I had Seen all things put to rights at the hotel, and the Doors closed and Shutters put up, I call all the Servants in the Bar-Room and treated them all around plentifull. and after drinking "the Yankees," healths," I paid each one according to Orders. I told them they could go just Where they pleased but be Sure the "Yankees," have no trubble finding them.

I then put the keys into my pocketts and proceeded to the Bank Where my old Mistress lived Who was hurridly packing her Silver-Spoons to go out in the Country,* to get away from the "Yankees." She asked Me with tears in her Eyes What was I going to do. I replyed I am going back to the Hotel now after you get through "Said She," child you better come and go out in the country with me, So as to keep away from the Yankees, Yes Madam "I replyed" I will come right back directly. I proceedeed down to Where Mrs Mazene lives (the Propietiors Wife) and deliverd the keys to her.

SAFE IN THE LINES

After delivering the hotel keys to Mrs Mazene I then Walked up Water St above Coalters Bridge Where I noticed a large crowd of the people Standing Eagerly gazeing across the River at a Small group of officers and Soilders who was now approaching the river Side and Immediately raised a flag of Truce and called out for Some one to come over to them. A White Man named James Turner, Stepped into a Small boat and went over to them. and after a few Minutes returned with Capt. Wood of Harris' Light Calvary, of New York. Who as Soon as he had Landed proceeded up the hill to the crowd amoung which Was the Mayor,* "Common Council," and the Corporation Attorney, Thomas Barton.

Capt Wood then in the name of Genl Auger, commanding the U.S.

Troops on the Falmouth Heights demanded the unconditional Surrender of its Town.* Old Lawer [Lawyer] Barton was bitterly opposed to Surrendering, Saying "the Confederacy had a plenty of Troops yet at their command." Then Why did they burn all the Bridges When We appeared on "Ficklins Heights?" demanded Capt Wood—Barton was Silent. "The Orders are "continued Capt Wood" that if any further attempt is made to burn Cotton or any thing else, or if any Trains of Cars Shall approach or attempt to leave the town Without permission of Genl Auger the Town Will be immediately fired upon.

The Mayor and "Common Council" hesitated no longer. Notwithstanding Lawer Barton's objection, and Capt Wood then Informed the Mayor that he would be required to come over to Genl Augers Headquarters the Next Morning at 10. 0.clock, and Sign the proper papers. He then bid them all good evening and having again entered the little Boat he Was Soon rowed across the River and in a few Minutes there after he was Seen mounted on horse back and being joined by Scores of other Horsemen, that had not been Seen While he was on our Side of the river. Evidently having been concealed in the Woods near by.

As Soon as the Officer had left the Constables was told to order the Negroes home Which they did, but While we dispersed from thereabout, a great many did not go home just then. I hastened off in the direction of home and after making a circutous route, I 'm in company with James Washington, my first Cusin and another free Colord Man, left the town near the Woolen Mills and proceeded up the road leading to Falmouth[,] Our object being to get right opposite the "Union Camp," and listen to the great number of "Bands" then playing those marching tunes, "the Star Spangled Banner," "Red White and Blue," etc.

We left the road just before we got to "Ficklin's Mill,"* and walked down to the river. The long line of Sentinels on the other Side doing duty colose to the Waters Edge.

Very Soon, one of a party of Soilders, in a boat call out to the crowd Standing arround Me do any of you want to come over—Every body "Said No." I hallowed out, "Yes I Want to come over." "All right—Bully for you," was the response. and they was Soon over to Our Side. I greeted them gladly and Stepped into their Boat. As Soon as James, Saw my determernation to go, he joines Me, and the other Young Man who had come along with us—

After we had landed on the other Side, a large crowd of the Soilders off duty, gathered around us and asked all kinds of questions in reference to the Whereabouts of the "Rebels" I had stuffed My pockets full of Rebel Newspapers and, I distributed them around as far as they would go greatly to the delight of the Men, and by this act Won their good opinions right away. I told them I was most happy to See them all that I had been looking for them for a long time. Just here" one of them asked me I Geuss you ain't a Secessish," then. Me "Said I," Why know [sic] Colord people ain't Secessh" why you ain't a Colord Man are you "Said he." Yes Sir I am "I replyed." and a Slave all my life. All of them Seemed to [be] utterly astonished. "So you Want to be free inquired one." by all Means "I answered." "Where is your Master? Said another. In the Rebel Navy, "I said." well you don't belong to any body then, "Said Several at once" the District of Columbia is free now. Emancapated 2 Days ago. I did not know what to Say, for I was dumb With Joy and could only thank God and Laugh. They insisted upon My going up to their camp on the Hill, and continued to ask all kinds of questions about the "rebs." I was conducted all over their camp and Shown Every thing that could interest me

Most kind attention Was Shown me by a Corporal in Company H, 21st New York State Volenteers. He Shared his meals and his bed with me and Seemed to pity me with all his Manly heart, his name was "Charles Ladd,"* But our aquaintance was of Short duration a few Weeks thereafter the army advanced and had Several Skirmishes and I never Seen him again.

It was near night before I thought of returning home (for though there was not as yet any of the "Union Troops" in Fredericksburg) the Town was right under their Guns and a close Watch was being kept on the Town.

When My friends (the Soilders) and Me arrived at the River Side We found the Boat drawn out of the Water and all Intercorse forbiden for the Night. My cousin and his friends had recrossed early in the afternoon.

So I found I Should have to remain with my new found friends for the Night. However I was well aquainted in Falmouth and Soon found the Soft Side of a Wooden Bench; at Mrs Butlers who had given up an outside room for the use of Some Soilders and 3 or 4 of us. A good fire was kept burning at night in an old fashiond fire-place.

A Most Memorable night that was to me the Soilders assured me that I was now a free man and had Nothing to do but to Stay With. They told me I could Soon get a Situation Waiting on Some of the officers. I had already been offered one or two, and had determined to take one or the other, as Soon as I could go over and get my cloths and Some $30.00 of my own.

Before Morning I had began to fee[l] like I had truly Escaped from the hands of the Slaves Master and With the help of God, I never Would be a Slave no more. I felt for the first time in my life that I could now claim Every cent that I should Work for as My own. I began now to feel that Life had a new joy awaiting me. I Might now go and come when I please So I wood remain With the army until I got Enough Money to travel further North This was the FIRST NIGHT of my FREEDOM. It was good Friday indeed the Best Friday I had ever Seen. Thank God—xxxx [in original]—We were all astir very early Next Morning for the Soilders had a Sad duty to perform. The night before they captured Falmouth, they, while advancing Suddenly in the darkness found the road Barracaded, and the Rebels concealed, close by who fired upon the advancing troops where the Road was cut through a hill and killed 7 and wounded Several.

The Funeral Was one of the most Solomn and impressive I had ever Witnessed in My Life before.* their company (Calvary) was dismounted and drawn up in line, around the Seven new graves, which had been dug Side-by Side

The old Family Burying ground wherein these New Made graves had been dug contained the Bones Some of the Oldest and Most wealthy of the Early Settlers of Falmouth. On Some of the Tombstones could be dimly traced The Birth-place of Some in England, Scotland and Wales as Well as Ireland. And amidst grand old Tombs and Vaults, sorrounded by Noble Ceders through Which the April Wind Seemed to moan low dirges, there they was now about to deposit the remains of (what the rebels was pleased to term) the low born "Yankee." Side-by-Side they rested those Seven coffins on the edge of these Seven New Made graves. While the Chaplins fervant pray[er] was wafted to the Skies and after a hymn (Windham) had been sung, those Seven Coffins was lowered to their final resting place. And amidst the Sound of the Earth falling into those New made Graves, the "Band of Harris Light Calvary broke forth in dear old "Pleyal Hymn. and when those graves were finished there was Scarcely a dry eye present.

And with heavy hearts their companions left that little Burrying ground Some Swearing to avenge their Deaths. A few hours after the funeral, the Mayor of Fredericks[burg] accompanied by Several of the Leading Men of the Town crossed the River and came to Headquarters, Where, the Town was formerly Surrendered. Troops was then Sent over to take possession of any thing Necessary for the "Union" Army* and to guard the Town. xxxxx [in original] About 3 weeks afterward I was Employed at the Headquarters of Majr Genl Rufus King, Who Was then commanding the 1st Division of "McDowells" Corps "Army of the Rappahannock," as Mess Servant I had left Genl Auger's Headquarters Some two Weeks, and was Staying with My old friend John Walters, at the "Phillips Farm," about 1 1/2 mile distant Eastward from Fredericksburg. Genl King had taken possession of the "Phillips House,"* Some 10 days previous, and one Sunday Morning While I was Strolling about the Yard of the Headquarters, looking at the Officers and Soilders, when I was accosted by Captain Charles Wood Aide-de-Camp to Genl King* as follows Well My Man Where do you live? "I have been living over there Sir." all my life. I Answered. Who did you belong to? Thomas R. Ware Sir." Where is he now? In the Rebel Navy on Board the Jamestown. "I replyed." Ah then you belong to me! "Said he Laughing. Thank you Sir, "Said I." tuching my hat" to which there was a general Laugh among them Standing by. The Captain after telling me I was free to do as I was pleased, then Engaged me at $18.00 per month to take charge of the General and his staff officers Mess and keep things in order generally.

I was conducted right to the Generals kitchen Where Every thing Was placed in my charge (after an Introduction of the cook, Whose name was Ransom Law;* Detailed from the 6th Wisconsin Regement as Cook) With an order to Make Some Beef Hash, Which the Officers, at Breakfast pronounced Splendid, much to my delight, for I had my fears of being able to please them.

But I Succeeded beyond my expectations and was soon a great favourite With all, from the General to the Orderlies.

One day soon after I was Employed and When I reported to him, "He said," John go to the Stable and tell Erastus (his hosteler) to give you My Horse Charley. Captain Wood wants you. I bowed and hastened to the Stable Where I found "Charley" Saddled and Bridled already. I Mounted and the Horse being a thourohh bred I was not a little frightened at his disposition to Walk on his hind feet, instead of all four. But as Soon as I could get him in hand and look about Myself, I discovered Captain Wood with a Company of Calvary awaiting a little distance off for Me to joine them. They then proceeded down the road toward Fredericksburg I was ordered to ride next to Captain Wood and Col Fairchilds, Who was riding by the Side of each other.

When we arrived at the "Old Ferry" oppisite the Town a Bridge had been nearly completed across, built on Old Canal boats a few Minutes delay and the last planks was laid. I now ascertained that I had been brought along to act as a *guide* in identifying the prominent Rebels of the Town, and after they had crossed the River and Entered the Town was proceeded directly to the Post-Office, then kept by one R. T. Thom. Capt Wood called me to point out Each place and to Name each person required. Mr Thom was then placed under arrest. Capt Wood then taken me and left all the Officers and Calvary, Except 2 Orderlies, and Said where is the "Sheakespeare House," this way Sir: And we Soon dismounted in front of the Hotel. He entered With me and gave Mrs Payton orders that Nothing Should be Sent out of that house, Except on an Order from Genl King

From there Capt Wood "rode to the Mayor of the Town, and other prominent Rebels, Some 25 or 30 in Number and the next morning they were Escorted to Headquarters under arrest* and were Sent to Washington City as prisiners. xx [in original]

COMMENTS ON CHAPTER 8

April 18th 1862, Was "Good-Friday." Washington correctly recalls the date when Union forces arrived on Stafford Hills for the first occupation of Fredericksburg, which lasted from 18 April to 31 August 1862. Some historians give a date for the troops' arrival several days later, but other first-hand accounts, such as those of Jane Howison Beale and Betty Maury, support Washington's memory. Beale's diary covers the years from 1850 to 1862, with scattered entries at first, then more detailed and frequent entries for 1861–1862. Her entry for 27 April 1862 notes: "Fredericksburg is a captured town, the enemy took possession of the

Stafford Hills . . . on Friday the 18th and their guns have frowned down upon us ever since, fortunately for us our troops were enabled to burn the bridges connecting our town with Stafford shore and thus saved us the presence of the Northern soldiers in our midst."[1]

Betty Maury's recollections complement Washington's. Maury, a dedicated Confederate partisan, recalled the night of 18 April with this entry in her diary: "Last night heard that enemy was 4 miles from Falmouth; Confed forces went across river to meet them; troops met strong force and retreated and fired the bridges; while dressing we saw great columns of smoke rising from the river. I went down to the river and shall never forget the scene there. Above were our three bridges, all in a light blaze from one end to the other and every few minutes the beams and timbers would splash into the water with a great noise. Below were two large steam boats, the Virginia and the St. Nicholas [a Yankee steamer that ran between Baltimore and Washington, D.C., which the Confederates had captured], and ten or twelve vessels all wrapt in flames. There were two or three rafts dodging in between the burning vessels containing families coming over to this side with the negros and horses."[2] Maury here seems to confirm that some slaveholders fled with their slaves.

The city council hastily made its own plans for dealing with the military threat. Due to the impending invasion by the Union, the clerk was to deposit the records and papers of the town in the vault of the clerk's office and was thereafter relieved of all responsibility for any damages to the records. The city council formed a committee to communicate with the Union commander. Since Confederate forces had evacuated the town, there would be no resistance. Revealing its doubt as much as its confidence, the council expressed its conviction that the safety of persons and property of the town would come under the "rules of civilized warfare." Defiant in the face of defeat, the council also declared Fredericksburg's sympathy and support for the government of Virginia and the Confederacy. It forbade the sale of alcohol to all troops and blacks. The penalty for violation of the ordinance on alcohol consumption was a twenty-dollar fine and jail not to exceed thirty days for white residents. "Negro or mulatto" violators would be punished by whipping not to exceed thirty-nine lashes and their liquor was to be destroyed. Police published and distributed handbills throughout the town announcing the ordinances.[3]

During the Civil War, as in the American Revolution, the society's underpinnings, values, and ideals came to the surface in different perceptions of what was being lost and gained. The Maury family women apparently saw the Confederacy as a bulwark of the patriarchal family and consequently viewed their losses as threats to that family tradition. In Maury's view, the men provided and protected, and during wartime their role as providers and protectors had come under attack. In the course of war, the women were to support the cause through their long-suffering sacrifices and unwavering devotion. Men were to take up arms.

Despite the unerring image of the patriarchal family as a series of reciprocal relationships extending from the master to women, children, and finally to the slaves, the war raised nagging doubts, not just about the loss of family property, but about family integrity, with the understanding that "family" must include everyone from masters down to slaves. On 25 April 1862, when the Yankee soldiers were building their bridges for the first assault on Fredericksburg and their presence in the town was seemingly everywhere, Maury expressed her greater concern that the "slaves will rise up" against their owners, an eventuality more to be feared than the Yankee soldiers.[4] It was not the fact that slaves would gain their freedom that upset her but the threat emancipation posed to the prevailing social order—at least how she and her ancestors had imagined and venerated it.[5]

Betty Maury admired and longed to emulate the longsuffering and devoted women in Richmond and Fredericksburg, who gave up their time to nurse the sick or sew for the soldiers, but did she overestimate the depths of Confederate nationalism among her southern peers? Unionism was substantial in the South, surprisingly prevalent in Fredericksburg, and even some members of her own family were Unionists. As noted elsewhere, Joseph Ficklin, the miller, adamantly opposed secession. On 22 April 1862, the *New York Herald* reported that Ficklin, "a wealthy citizen of Falmouth, whose loyalty has rendered him exceedingly obnoxious to the rebels, invited [Union Brigadier] General [Christopher Colon] Augur into his mansion, and entertained the staff and other officers with a bounteous repast."[6] Later, when Ficklin filed a claim for war damages and asked for compensation on the basis of his unionism, local supporters included two merchants, a homebuilder, a farmer, and several millwrights, all Unionists themselves who testified in Ficklin's behalf. John Minor and Mary Minor Blackford, Betty's cousins, were antislavery advocates, whom Betty labeled "eccentric people."[7]

Despite the impressive expressions of dissent in the midst of a place more well known for its smashing defeat of the Union forces, Fredericksburg appears to have had no difficulty raising men to fight for the Confederacy. It would be misleading to sum up antislavery, antisecessionist, and antiwar sentiment in the town, place it on a scale, and balance the beam in favor of the Union. Besides, the situation was far more complex. With Lincoln's call for troops, as most historians have long recognized, those on the southern fence chose the Confederacy, even though some still held on to their antislavery and Unionist beliefs.

The Yankees turned out to be the 1st Brigade of "Kings Division." Other accounts of conditions in the town upon the arrival of the Union army verify Washington's recollections. Washington recalls here the initial advance of the Army of Virginia south toward Richmond. General Augur's forces set out in March 1862, under the command of Irvin McDowell, taking Falmouth across the Rappahannock River on 16 April. Falmouth sat north of Fredericksburg, and just below where the Rappahannock takes a sharp turn south. The military campaign was part of the Lincoln administration's strategy to move on the Confederate capitol of Richmond in order to bring the war to a quick and decisive conclusion.[8] The Union army had superior forces and easily overwhelmed Fredericksburg's defenses. On 17 April, one Fredericksburg woman recalled, "Our forces retreated yesterday, and now not a Confederate flag, soldier, or tent can be seen. . . . It was the saddest sight I ever saw, to see our men retreating yesterday, almost at double quick, leaving us behind to the enemy, and the black smoke rolling up from the burning bridges." The correspondent expressed her fears of what the Union army would do and wrote that the Confederate forces "sent a white flag over yesterday and we sent some men with one back to them. Then two Yankees came over and said, 'Gen. Augur (their Gen.) said he would take possession of the city at eleven oclock today and that private property should be respected,' but who believes a word they say[?] We tried to hide every thing we could yesterday."[9] The Fredericksburgers whom Washington served took similar measures while slaves secretly rejoiced.

My old Mistress . . . was hurridly packing her Silver-Spoons to go out in the Country. This extraordinary scene speaks volumes about the two different worlds that slaves and owners occupied. One of the first concerns of slave owners faced with imminent invasion was property, typically silver and slaves. Notice, as Washington does, that Taliaferro reminds Washington of his status as a "child" in her care and how she attempts to scare him into her control.

As Soon as he had Landed proceeded up the hill to the crowd amoung which Was the Mayor. Montgomery Slaughter, the mayor of Fredericksburg during the Civil War, resided in a two-story wood frame house on the corner of Princess Anne and Amelia streets. He was forty-two years old in 1860 and listed his occupation on the census as "merchant/miller." He had real estate valued at $18,000 and a personal estate of $20,000. He headed a large household that included Eliza Slaughter, thirty-four; William, thirteen; Mary, nine; Fanny, seven; Montgomery, Jr., four; Philip, two; Charles, eight months; and James Swetman, a 23-year-old clerk with real estate valued at $5,000 and a personal estate of $16,000. Slaughter owned at least thirteen slaves: a 55-year-old black female, a 45-year-old black female, a 35-year-old mulatto female, a 34-year-old black female, a 32-year-old black male, a 23-year-old black male, a 23-year-old black female, a 12-year-old black female, a 10-year-old black male, a 9-year-old black female, a 6-year-old black male, a 5-year-old black female, and a 6-month-old black female.[10]

Capt Wood then in the name of Genl Auger . . . demanded the unconditional Surrender of its Town. The commander whose orders Captain Wood carried out that day was Christopher C. Augur, who graduated West Point in 1843 and served with distinction during the Mexican-American War. Augur participated in actions against Indians in Oregon in the mid-1850s, and when the Civil War broke out, he was called east, promoted to brigadier general of volunteers, and in November 1861 given command of a brigade in Irvin McDowell's corps assigned to defend Washington, D.C. In July 1862, Augur was given a division under the command of Nathaniel P. Banks. Following his service in the Rappahannock campaign, Augur was severely wounded at the battle of Cedar Mountain, Virginia, after which he was promoted to major general of volunteers.[11]

We left the road just before we got to "Ficklin's Mill." Joseph B. Ficklin was a successful Fredericksburg-Falmouth businessman. He owned the Bridgewater Mills, the Falmouth toll bridge, and real estate in Fredericksburg. He was also president of the new Bank of Commerce. In 1822, Joseph B. Ficklin and Sons had established one of the most significant milling operations in the area. The Bridgewater Mills consisted of a large elevator, a mill with a housed wheel, and numerous associated buildings. The mill sat at the lower raceway just south of the Falmouth bridge. Its power derived from part of the canal system. Ficklin was the first miller in America to produce a "family" brand flour. It won the first silver medal at the 1887 Paris exposition and at the Atlanta exposition the same year. Bridgewater had the capacity to produce about 150 barrels of flour and 400 bushels of meal per day by the late nineteenth century. Fire severely damaged the mill in 1858, but it was quickly rebuilt. It produced ten grades of flour, "Ficklin's Superlative" being the highest grade. It also ground corn into meal and produced animal feeds.[12]

More interesting, perhaps, in a region where secessionist sentiment ran high was Ficklin's politics. Although largely unknown at the time except by a few people with whom he had contact, but confirmed by the records of the Southern Claims Commission (a postwar commission established to investigate claims of property losses by southern Unionists), Ficklin was a courageous and devoted supporter of the Union, despite his birth in neighboring Culpeper County and his ownership of twenty-seven slaves. During the investigation of his claim by the Claims Commission, Ficklin testified and deponents verified that Ficklin had attempted to vote against secession in Virginia. The stakes for actually voting against secession were very high in 1861 since avowed Unionists made tempting targets for secessionist partisans impatient with those who refused to fight for their cause. Ficklin lived with his wife and family in an eighteenth-century house known as Belmont, purchased in 1825, that overlooked the Rappahannock River. He had six children from two marriages. He died in 1874 and was buried in Fredericksburg. During the war, he helped his sons escape through enemy lines to avoid the draft and infuriated local partisans on one occasion by giving only ten dollars—though he had considerable wealth—to support the Confederacy, when a group of local women called on his mill for donations.[13]

His name was "Charles Ladd." Charles Ladd of Hoosick, New York, enlisted in Company H of the Thirtieth New York Infantry on 3 May 1861, just weeks after Lincoln's 15 April call for 75,000 federal troops in response to the Confederate assault on Fort Sumter, South Carolina, on 11 April. Son of a harness maker, Ladd served with distinction.[14] The Thirtieth New York Infantry left camp guarding Washington, D.C., on 10 March 1862, and marched with the "Iron Brigade"—First Brigade, First Division, First Corps—of the Army of the Potomac to Manassas, and from there to Falmouth and Massaponax, several miles south of Fredericksburg. Ladd's company was then moved to Front Royal in the Shenandoah Valley. There in the spring of 1862, Confederate general Thomas J. "Stonewall" Jackson was threatening the federal capital as a way to divert Union forces gathering for an assault on Richmond. President Lincoln had ordered Union general George B. McClellan to chase Jackson and his Confederates, which disrupted McClellan's planned invasion. Washington's friend was called out of Fredericksburg to join in that pursuit, which had the effect of stalling the Union advance to Richmond. Ladd survived the Valley campaign of 1862 and was transferred to Company Battery G of the Fifth New York Light Artillery Regiment on 13 November 1862. After the war, Ladd settled in Fulton, New York, and took up his father's trade. By 1870 he was married with a two-year-old son.[15]

The Funeral Was one of the most Solomn and impressive I had ever Witnessed in My Life before. Good Friday 1862 was 18 April, the day after Fredericksburg fell to Union forces. That Saturday, funerals took place for the soldiers Washington mentioned, who fell at Falmouth on 16 April. The Fredericksburg resident who lamented the capture of her town on 17 April, cited above, also mentioned the skirmish to which Washington alludes. "The enemy took Falmouth yesterday," wrote the sister of Samuel S. Brooke, a Fredericksburg resident and lieutenant in the Forty-seventh Virginia, on 17 April. She feared for her safety and wrote that the Union general had given assurances that locals' property would not be taken, but she despaired that the Confederate army had melted away so quickly. "Our force is said to have been [3,200?], the Yankees are estimated at from 15,000 to 800[0?]. We had some skirmishing with them and lost a man or two, several men wounded, we killed several of the enemy."[16]

The comparatively small skirmish north of Fredericksburg stands in the shadow of larger events. On the same day—16 April—that Falmouth fell to Union forces, the Confederate states' government adopted conscription. Earlier that month the Union had begun the Peninsular campaign to take Richmond, and General McClellan began the push toward Richmond with Yorktown, Virginia—the site of General Charles Cornwallis's 1781 surrender to George Washington, which ended the Revolutionary War. The siege had begun on 5 April, but Yorktown would not fall until 6 May. On 7–8 April, meanwhile, the Union army under the command of Ulysses S. Grant prevailed over the Confederate forces, led by Albert Sydney Johnston and Pierre G. T. Beauregard, at Shiloh on the Tennessee River near the Mississippi border. The battle of Shiloh showed the extreme costs of pitched battles between armies using rifled muskets and sophisticated artillery. Casualties included 23,741 killed, wounded, or missing on both sides—more than all casualties of the Revolutionary War, War of 1812, and Mexican-American War combined.[17] Despite the tremendous costs of victory, a soldier in the Iron Brigade camped near Fredericksburg wrote at the time that Shiloh was a "glorious victory to our army." Recording the actual death of Confederate general Johnston and the supposed death of Beauregard (he would live another sixty-one years), the soldier concluded that "it raises the brooding spirits of many engaged in the war."[18]

Troops was then Sent over to take possession of any thing Necessary for the "Union" Army. The spring rains fell steadily around the time the Union forces took Fredericksburg, and restless soldiers sent to find provisions for the army sometimes preyed on civilians. Provost Marshal General Marsena Rudolph Patrick, who was responsible for policing soldiers' conduct in the Army of the Potomac, observed the situation in Fredericksburg several days after it fell. Patrick complained that soldiers "demoralized from this long inaction from Rain" were "Strolling in all directions" and getting into trouble. "They, or some of our Command," he continued, "have been plundering houses, insulting women & committing depredations for miles around the country." The provost marshal despaired of making good soldiers out of some men with questionable backgrounds. "I am almost discouraged," he wrote on 21 April, "in my efforts to get thieves, skulks and political scribblers to become Soldiers."[19] Patrick's mention of "political scribblers" was probably an oblique criticism of General Rufus King, his division commander, who had been a newspaper editor before the war. King likely employed men in the army who had worked for newspapers back in Wisconsin, and West Point–trained General Patrick's dim view of newspaper reporters may also reflect the prevailing opinion that men who covered the rough-and-tumble world of party politics were not professionals. Whatever the civilian occupation of Union soldiers posted in and around Fredericksburg, the fears of local citizens concerning their security and property were not unfounded. The Union army was not there—explicitly—to free slaves either, and Washington had to be wary of the soldiers in whose camps he sought refuge.

Genl King had taken possession of the "Phillips House." Phillips House was an important landmark of the Civil War. Washington served there in the spring of 1862, but by the winter of the same year it would be used as a command post. Phillips House served as Union general Ambrose Burnside's headquarters before and during the battle of Fredericksburg in December 1862. The house was across the Rappahannock River at Falmouth Station, and until the original structure went up in flames on 14 February 1862, it was a large farmhouse overlooking the river and Fredericksburg to its south and west. Several days after the Union defeat at Fredericksburg, the *Richmond Daily Dispatch* reported that "Gen. Burnside was at the Phillips House nearly all day. His position most of the time was on the upper balcony, where, with a powerful glass, he was watching the movements across the river. He has his staff and couriers running to and fro, conveying orders, and bringing reports of the progress of the fight. He gave orders with promptitude and succinctly." Colonel Samuel K. Zook of the Fifty-seventh New York Infantry mentioned in his official report of the battle that "At 7 a.m. of the 11th" of December, "the Fifty-third Pennsylvania, Second Delaware, and Fifty-second New York having been formed, with the Twenty-seventh Connecticut, near the camp of the latter, on the Stafford Court House road, took up the line of march about 8 a.m., in rear of the Irish Brigade for a point near the Phillips house, where they bivouacked, having been joined by the Fifty-seventh and Sixty-sixth New York during the after-noon." Many of those men spent their last night alive camped out beside the farmhouse where the Union command was planning what would be one of the most disastrous battles of the Civil War.

Phillips House figured in the battle of Chancellorsville the following May. The Union forces under General John Sedgwick used it as an ob-servation center, monitoring enemy movements from it with a telescope and setting up a signal station and a telegraph. The Union strategy fell apart after General Stonewall Jackson surprised the main body of Union troops under General Joseph Hooker at Chancellorsville—a few miles west of Fredericksburg—on 2 May. Hooker's forces retreated to defen-sive positions before a smaller Confederate army that Lee and Jackson split to surprise Hooker on his right flank. On the night of 2 May, Gen-eral Jackson was shot and wounded by his own pickets, and he died on 10 May. Meanwhile, Sedgwick's Union troops, split off from Hooker's forces, tried to take Fredericksburg but were quickly outmaneuvered and attacked from the west, south, and east on 5 May. On the night of 5–6 May, Sedgwick withdrew across the river in the direction of Phil-

Phillips House, a major landmark of the Civil War. From *Civil War Photographs, 1861–1865* (Washington, D.C.: Library of Congress, 1977), no. 0173.

lips House. It was a crushing victory for the Union forces under Hooker, and although Lee lost his most audacious general, the victory helped to persuade Lee to go on the offensive and invade Maryland and Pennsylvania, which set the stage for the battle of Gettysburg. A white farmhouse stands on the site of Phillips House, and at least one outbuilding from the nineteenth century is still standing.[20]

I was accosted by Captain Charles Wood Aide-de-Camp to Genl King. It is possible, but improbable, that the aide-de-camp to whom Washington refers was Charles Wood of Watertown, Wisconsin. At sixteen, that Charles Wood, a farmer's son, volunteered, and on 6 June 1861, he enlisted in Company B of the Fifth Infantry Regiment, which left Wisconsin under the command of General Rufus King on 24 July. That September, General Winfield Scott Hancock took command of the Fifth Wisconsin, which was incorporated into the Second Division, Sixth Corps of the U.S. Army. It took part in the Peninsular campaign, including the battle of Williamsburg on 5 May 1862. Wood was promoted to full lieutenant on 8 March 1864, in the year he turned nineteen, and was discharged on the same day. In addition to the battle of Williamsburg, the Fifth Wisconsin was also involved in the battles of Antietam, Fredericksburg, Gettysburg, the Wilderness, and Spotsylvania Courthouse and the siege of Petersburg. The same Charles Wood survived the war and settled in Ellsworth, Wisconsin, where the 1870 census taker recorded him working as a carpenter and married to a nineteen-year-old woman named Mary.[21]

The general whom Washington served was Rufus King. After attending the preparatory department of Columbia College—where his father was president—King was graduated from the United States Military Academy in 1833 and appointed to the engineer corps; he resigned his commission in 1836 and became assistant engineer of the New York & Erie Railroad. After resigning from the railroad in 1839, he was briefly adjutant general of New York before becoming associate editor of the *Albany Evening Journal* and the *Albany Advertiser* from 1841 to 1845. He relocated to Wisconsin in 1845 and for the next sixteen years served as editor of the *Milwaukee Sentinel*. He was active in framing that state's 1848 constitution. King also served as superintendent of Milwaukee's public schools from 1849 to 1861 and held a variety of other posts, including member of the board of visitors governing the U.S. Military

Academy. President Lincoln appointed him U.S. ambassador to the papal states, but he resigned that post after Fort Sumter fell in April 1861 and organized the "Iron Brigade," which included the Second, Sixth, and Seventh Wisconsin Infantry, among other units. The same year he was commissioned brigadier general of Wisconsin volunteers, and after he received a commission in the U.S. Army, King's forces were posted in defense of Washington, D.C., from May 1861 to March 1862.

Like many of the forces defending Washington, King's division was ordered to "cover" the capital while advancing toward Richmond, since the bulk of the Army of the Potomac was involved in the Peninsular campaign in eastern Virginia. When John Washington encountered his forces, King was commanding a division of General Irvin McDowell's Third Corps, which was occupying the Rappahannock until Confederate forces under Stonewall Jackson began the Shenandoah Valley campaign to draw Union forces from the Peninsula. After the capture of Fredericksburg, King's division was ordered north, and McDowell posted his division at Gainesville in Prince William County, Virginia, in order to prevent a Confederate army under General James Longstreet from joining his comrade Stonewall Jackson in the events leading to the Battle of Second Bull Run, 28–30 August 1862.

Inexplicably, and without orders, King pulled back from his position, which compelled the pullback of a division under Union general James Ricketts at nearby Thoroughfare Gap. Ricketts' move allowed Longstreet's Confederates unimpeded passage through Thoroughfare Gap, and at a critical moment they joined Jackson's right flank then under assault from General John Pope's forces.

Meanwhile, on 29 August, King's forces fought valiantly at Groveton, Virginia, just south of Alexandria, but his mistake set the stage for the Union disaster at Second Bull Run (also known as Second Manassas). On 30 August, General Pope attacked Jackson's forces, apparently without knowing that General Longstreet had reinforced him. After massed Confederate artillery repulsed a Union assault by General Fitz John Porter's forces, Longstreet's army of 28,000 Confederates counterattacked in the largest simultaneous mass assault of the war. That assault crushed the Union left flank, and Pope's army retreated to Bull Run, site of the first battle of Manassas the previous year. Pope fought a valiant rearguard action, but quickly retreated to Centreville. On 1 September, the Confederate commander Robert E. Lee ordered his armies to follow Pope's retreating army, thereby seizing the momentum built by the surprise at Second Manassas. King was later posted to Manassas, but he was relieved of command and his actions at Gainesville were determined to have been an act of willful disobedience and a "grave error."

In an ironic twist, King was reassigned to a court-martial which was to try Fitz John Porter for his role in the horrible losses of Second Manassas, "thus," according to one historian, "affording the rather unusual spectacle of a military officer reprimanded for dereliction sitting in judgment upon another officer charged with the loss of the same battle." By April 1863, he was given command of forces holding Yorktown, Virginia. He later commanded a division holding Fairfax Court House, Virginia. Failing health compelled him to resign on 20 October 1863. He returned home to New York City, where he held several positions including deputy collector of customs; he died there on 13 October 1867.[22]

An Introduction of the cook, Whose name was Ransom Law. Ransom Law was a 26-year-old painter and native New Yorker living in Appleton, Wisconsin, with his wife Sarah and toddler Charles when the census was taken in 1860.[23] He enlisted as a private in Company E of the Sixth Wisconsin Infantry Regiment on 28 June 1861, twelve days after it was organized. As part of the Iron Brigade, the Sixth Wisconsin saw action in most of the major battles in Maryland and Virginia from 1861 to 1865, including Second Bull Run, Antietam, Fredericksburg, Chancellorsville, Gettysburg, the Wilderness, Cold Harbor, and the battle of the Five Forks. The Iron Brigade lost more than twice as many soldiers to war wounds as to disease—exactly the reverse ratio of fatalities from wounds to disease among Civil War regiments as a whole. Law was wounded on 29 April 1863 at Fitzhugh Crossing, Virginia, near Chancellorsville, and received a disability discharge from the U.S. Army on 26 June. After the war, Law moved his family to Illinois. In 1870, he was living with his wife and 13-year-old son in Chicago's Seventh Ward, working as a letter carrier.[24]

The Mayor of the Town, and other prominent Rebels, Some 25 or 30 in Number . . . were Escorted to Headquarters under arrest. Although the date is not given and the number does not agree, this account seems to be a reference to the August 1862 arrest of nineteen prominent Fredericks-burgers—merchants, lawyers, the mayor, a newspaper editor, a pastor, a wealthy farmer, a tailor, a carpenter, and others—who were held in Old Capitol prison in Washington, D.C., for six weeks before they were released.[25]

9

On the Move with the Union Army

Gen King Soon, after the incidents narrated in the proceeding chapter Stationed his headquarters in Fredericksburg at My old Home "The Farmers Bank," and as a Natural consequence Every body and Every thing seemed to take new life. There were Some few Rebel Simithizers among the Colord people But they kept very quite [sic].

Hundreds of Colord people obtained papers and free transportation to Washington and the North, and Made their Escape to the Free States Day after day the Slaves came into camp and Every where that the "Stars and Stripes" Waved they Seemed to know freedom had dawned to the Slave.

May 23rd "The Battle of Front Royal" Was fought and Genl King was ordered to March to "Catletts Station," on the Orange and Alexandria Railroad about 38 Miles from Fredericksburg, Whence a part of the Division was transported by Railroad to Front Royal but in consequence of an accident on the Railroad by which Several Soilders Was killed and Wounded, the remaining Troops, With the General and his Staff and followers had to march overland to Hay Market, distant 17 miles—the Servants horses had been Sent on the last and there being no Extra Horses John Brown (The Generals hostler) and Me and Several other (Colord) Men had to foot it with the Soilders.

There Was Several Regiments of Infantry and Calvary, along with the Headquarters Wagons and Transports but all to heavy laden to give us a ride for a few Minutes.

Many of the Soilders laughed at us and cherred to See us dismounted as Well as they. We left "Catletts Station," about 3. o clock in the afternoon the Weather Was very pleasant but cloudy. We Were hurried across fields and Meadows and by paths along rugged roads and through the Yards of Farm Houses. While the terified Women and children huddled together (White and Colord) as if for protection from the invading foe. About 10. o clock that night we halted and camped for the Night. Major Coons was in command of a company of Harris Light Calvary,* and Our Headquarters trains, and Soon as the Soilders pitched their tents John Brown

Me and 4 of the Generals Orderlies who was also dismounted and all of us Without tents began to look about for Some Shelters of Some kind.

We had pass a little farm House about a Mile back, And as it had began to rain quite hard, Some one proposed that we go back and take Shelter in one of the Out houses, Which was agreed to and We were Soon Searching all the buildings for Some occupant, but we found the place entirely deserted. We Soon Made a fire in a lower Room and proceeded to Make Coffe and then to Make our Supper off of "hardTack," and Some Salt pork, While we sat partaking of Our Needed repast. We were Suddenly alarmed by hearing a horse dash into the yard and Some one in a loud Voice demand What We Were! and what We Were doing here

Seizing our pistols and Sabres haistly and looking out the door, we found Major Coons and a Squad of Cavalry at his heels, he Swearing "like a trooper," ordered Us into camp instantly and not to leave again on Perial of Death.

We obeyed and followed into camp, Which was dark and Silent as the grave.

The Camp was a Marsh Wet Spot coverd with coarse grass near a Creek. the grass was too Wet to lie on if it could be avoided—after a Whisperd consultation (no one Was allowed to talk loud) We again one by one glided Silently out of camp skirtirt the feels [skirting the fields?] reached the little Farm House. After Having been told the "Gurrilas," had been there the Night before and captured Some of our Men. and pulling an old Bedstead to peices and with one or two fence rails Secured the two Doors, We laid Our Napsacks on the floor against Each Door for pillows and Our pistols under our heads and our Sabres close by for immediate Use in case of an attack, during the night. We were Soon in a Sound Slumber, Sweet and refreshing from Which We did not awake until about 6. o clock Next Morning.

One of the boys in the mean time had unfastened the Door and on looking over to the Camp was not a little Surprised to find Every Man and beast gone. And Worse than all the fallen rain had hid every trace of the direction the troops had taken.

Following the road Northward Was our only hope, and With our unusal good chance of being captured by "Mosby and his gang" of gurillas*—Late in the after noon we came up with the rear of the army near

Haymarket. parsueing the road onward We found Genl King and his Staff at a Tavern in the Village.

The General had Just given Orders to the Headquarters trains to go on to Gainesville on the Orange and Alexandria R.R. Where We encamped for a few days during which it rained Most of the time.

Early one morning on the fourth day I think, We received Marching orders to Warrenton, the road a turnpike was an unusal good one for this Location, being Well settled with Stone, over which the Wagons ambulances and troops, moved with comparative ease the day was a beautiful one. and the road was dotted here and there with fine and Stately old mansions, Surround by growing wheat and corn fields, and every indication for Wealth and prosperity.

About 3. o clock in the Afternoon We arrived in Site of Warrenton and Entered the Town. General King at the head of his Division With Bands playing "The Star Spangled Banner" "Red White and Blue," etc. etc.—

Crowds of Rebels Stood on the Court-House Steeps and looked vengance at us as We advanced in to the Town. General King, established his Headquarters in the Town at the Warren Green Hotel. The Troops encamped outside of the Town on the heights—The Scenery is beautiful around this town: Mountains Hills and Valleys, being covered with Splendid vegetation this season of the year.—The "Fauquiers white Sulphure Springs," is located only a few mils from this place, and was much frequented before the War by the Wealthy in Search of health and enjoyment during the Sumer.

The Officers and Servants had very good rooms assigned to them during our Stay here, the hotel furnishing all necessary accomadations. Our Stay was of Short duration, however. We arrived on Wednesday, and Sunday Morning Some of us went to a church on one of the Main Streets, where one of Our Chaplins was to preach.

The opening hymn had been sung a prayer and chapter read, when and orderly Was Seen to approach the pulpit, with a letter or order in his hand—which he handed to the chaplin and hastily retired.

After reading it the chaplin arose and Said" Every Man is hereby ordered, to report to his respective quarters immediately. That was enough! when the church was left—the first news that we herd was "the rebs is advancing" xx [in original]. In two hours the camps was all broken up. The Headquarters evacuated and the *Calvary* advancing toward "Catlett Station" again.

It was about 3 o,clock p.m. When the General with his Stall [sic] and followers left the Town amidst the prayers and good will of the colord people that remained behind.

Hundreds of Colord Men, Women, and children followed us closly on foot.* Poor Mothers with their babys at their breasts, Fathers with a few cloths in Bundles or larger children accompanying them followed close in the foot steps of the Soilders Seeming to think this would be their Surrist Way to freedom. The distance from Warrenton to Catletts Station was 12 miles and these poor Souls would be permitted to go to Washington Where they were provided for by the U.S. government as "contrabands of War" So they would be Sent down free of cost by the Railroad.—We camped just below "Catletts Station" that night. and resuming our March next Morning camped at our old Headquarters oppisite Fredericksburg at the "Phillips House."

But a few days after We were ordered across to Fredericksburg and made the Headquarters in the "Farmers Bank,"* My old home again this afforded me a great pleasure of being back with old Friends, my grandmother and aunt lived there and kept thing together for the old mistriss hid away in the country.

I Occupied my old room for the first Since I had Escaped. and I Surely Was never So happy as then and probably Will not soon forget it soon— Genl McClellan was advancing on Richmond from Fortress Monroe, about this time. and Soon the Orders Was given to advance from our Headquarters When "Gibbons Brigade" was Sent on as far as Milford Depot and Bowling Green. Genl Kirkpatrick Was Making things lively With his calvary every now and then and capturing prisoners and arms.

We were awaiting marching orders, When one day, a dispatch was Sent hastily recalling the the [sic] advanced troops and ordering the Evacuation of Fredericksburg* and an immediate advance to Culpeper Court House.

COMMENTS ON CHAPTER 9

Major Coons was in command of a company of Harris Light Calvary. The Harris Light Cavalry was raised under the patronage of U.S. senator

Ira Harris of New York in response to the successes of the Confederate "Black Horse Cavalry" in the first Bull Run campaign of 1861. Under the War Department's authority, the Harris Light Cavalry made up the Sixth Regiment of the New York Cavalry, though it was first known as the "Ira Harris Guard." Most of the Harris Light Cavalry were supporting General George B. McClellan's siege on Yorktown at this time, but at least one squadron of the battalion "participated in the movements in front of Washington," according to the regimental history. That probably means that the company of the Harris Light Cavalry Washington encountered under Major Coons was participating in the movement "covering" Washington, D.C., from possible Confederate assault in April 1862 while the main body of the Army of the Potomac pressed ahead to the southeast on the Peninsula between the York and James rivers in the direction of Richmond.[1] Fredericksburg was on the rail route about halfway between Richmond and Washington, D.C.

"Mosby and his gang" of gurillas. John Singleton Mosby, a hot-tempered Virginian who had shot a fellow student during his time at the University of Virginia, was at the beginning of the war an enlisted soldier in the First Virginia Cavalry. Insubordinate to the colonel of his regiment, he left but was able to join General J. E. B. Stuart's staff as a scout and was commissioned a lieutenant. During the Peninsular campaign that included taking Fredericksburg, he made possible Stuart's famous "Ride around McClellan," which embarrassed the Union army and rallied Confederates. Mosby was captured but released in July 1862 in a prisoner exchange, after which he rejoined Stuart and was given the opportunity to raise a partisan cavalry band for use in disrupting Union activities in and around Loudoun County in northern Virginia. That assignment befitted Mosby's restless temperament, and he soon earned the name "Gray Ghost" for his audacious raids. As head of a partisan battalion, he disrupted Union supply lines and compelled field commanders to send large numbers of troops to protect their lines of supply and communication. He threatened the Union armies guarding Washington, D.C. His audacity won him acclaim from Confederates and inspired fear among Unionists like Washington. In March 1863 he rode into Fairfax Court House with a force of twenty-nine men and entered Union general Edwin H. Stoughton's tent, allegedly awaking him with a slap to the general's

rear. Mosby's disruption of supply lines and communications so irritated Union commanders that Union general Philip Sheridan threatened to summarily execute any partisan ranger who was caught. Mosby's guerrillas disbanded after Lee surrendered to Grant in April of 1865; Mosby died fifty-one years later, in 1916.[2]

Hundreds of Colord Men, Women, and children followed us closly on foot. Washington's account gives ample evidence that as the Union army advanced in the South, slaves and their families took the opportunity to escape behind Union lines. The men often attempted to join the military forces, while the women and children followed along as "contraband of war."

We were ordered across to Fredericksburg and made the Headquarters in the "Farmers Bank." Between April and August 1862, the Farmers' Bank was an important Union logistical center. Union general Marsena Patrick established his headquarters there in April while acting as military governor of Fredericksburg.[3]

A dispatch was Sent hastily recalling the . . . advanced troops and ordering the Evacuation of Fredericksburg. Fredericksburg passed back and forth between Union and Confederate control before the famous battle in December 1862 when the Confederate forces enjoyed one of their greatest victories of the war.

10

Unwelcome Home

Sunday Morning August 10th 1862 dawned bright and warm, and the indications of a Warm day Was apparent to every one, the Whole Division Was moving around Falmouth Va and Calvary, Artillary, Infintary, and Wagons and Ambulances was filling the roads that led toward Culpeper County. Information had reached Our army that Gen Banks had been attacked at or near "Ceder Mountain," in Culpeper County. and We were hastening to reinforce him. Genl John A. Pope was then in charge of the Army of Virginia. and his Headquarters Was near Banks. xxxxx [in original]

On leaving the camp at Falmouth Our Division March rapidly to "Ellis'" Ford Where they Forded the river. the Infantry devesting themselves of their pants and Water not being over Waist deep there.

We found the ford guarded by the 106th New York Regiment. Our General Stoped here from about Sunset until 2. o.clock at Night: Some of Our boys went to the Kitchen belonging to "Ellis'" and tried to purchase Some Hot Biscuit Which the colord Women were bakeing for Sale but the Door Was guarded by the New York Men, Who had orders not to let our men enter. So our Boys thought they Would get even With them and later in the Night Some half dozen of them Enterd the Mill and after Stealing about 30 fine Hams, turned the Water on, and left the Mill running Without any thing to grind. About 2 o.clock that night whisperd orders was given for us to Mount. and after crossing the river, day broke and found us Miles away from "Ellis'" Mill.

As the Sun arose above the Mountains, the air loaded with the Sick perfume of clover and Wild flowers. and the heavy Mountain dew looking like drops of Silver on the rich leaves and blossoms.

We had ridden past regiment after regiment of our men, and the General and his Staff was almost out of Sight a little a head, there being a turn in the road Just there, I was looking around at the beautiful mountain Scenery around me. Each Side of the road being thickly lined with low ceder and pine. When I was Suddenly Startled by the report of a Rifle near by and the Whistle of a "Minnie" ball close to my head.

I drove the spurs into my horses' flanks and hurried forward to rejoin our men.

We were now nearing the Battle field, and we Were in Momentary Expectation of an attack.

About 3. o,clock General King and his Staff halted at "Strasburg" for a rest and Lunch. While resting here the General called me and Sent me back to the wagon train for Some Whiskey that was on hand, put up in pint flasks.

I rode back and found the train about 2 Miles in the rear awaiting Orders to move onward. After obtaining the whiskey, I hastened back to Strausburg and found the General and his Staff, had Just rode off toward Ceder Mountain. It Was now about 5. o,cl and following the direction they had gone I Soon ascertained they had left the Main Road and Crossed the fields from Strausburg to Ceder Mountain (about 10 miles) the road was packed crowded and jammed with Calvary, Artillery, infinty [infantry] Wagons, Contrabands, refugees and cattle. I pressed my horse on toward the front, passing Brigades and regiments until I had overtaken the Artillery Which was in advance. Night had now overtaken us now I Received Orders not to advance any further than the Artillery, as they were feeling their Way, to avoid a Surprise by night. The Reble picketts had been driven in Earley in the Evening—

Woods on both Sides of the road here Was densely thick and we did not know what moment the Rebels Might fire on us.

We Soon approached a part of the road that was fenced in with a rough Stone Wall of Great thickness and about 4 or 4½ feet high the order Was passed (in Whispers) to dismount and lye down on the ground Which was done and We remained in that position for Some time.

Finally the Order to mount came in whispers. A portion of the Wall had been removed in order to let the artillery, and Wagons, and Calvary pass in Several places. After advancing Some distance up a hill We came to a halt and camped for the Night. Soon after we got orders to water the horses and in Squads, We proceeded to a little Stream not far off and Watered our horses. I also filled my canteen with Water and drank freely of it, and learned afterward that the Spring from Which it ran, had been poisoned a few days before. The only Effects I felt from it was rather Violent pains, with a burning thirst. I fed my horse and Slept in an ammunition Wagon that night up[on] Boxes of Bumb—Shells.

Early next Morning I rode off in Search of Genl King. and found him and his Staff after a few Minutes ride where he had a kind of Shelter Made of Green Corn Stalks, from a field just across the road.

A few hours after I arrived Our Headquarters teams came up and we pitched into the hams Sliced and by Sticking a Stick through the Slices Soon broiled enough for a good Meal by holding it to the fire.

A few Shells from the rebels Soon put an end to our cooking by the Smoke from our fire Serving them as a Mark.

During this afternoon we received orders to fall back to "Fleet's farm Where the General established his headquarters for the time being in close proximity to Gen John Pope's Headquarters Gen Shields and Gen Banks Major Genl Pope being then in command of the "Army of Virginia." great preparations were being Made for Some important Move. Orders had Just been issued for the Discharge of all Servants Except hostlers and Cooks.* Of course this did not effect my case.

But A Reward of $300.00 had been offered for my head in Fredericksburg* and knowing if I Should be captured by the rebels I Should be taken to Richmond Va Where I was well known and no doubt be immediately hung or Shot for being With the "Yankees."

I therefore obtained permission to Visit Fredericksburg going by Way of Washington City.

Genl King willingly gave the desired permission now, as there was no fighting going on just then. The Hospitals at Culpeper Cte. was crow[d]ed with the Wounded, and the Dead had been burried from the last Battle field.

The Stars and Stripes waved proudly from the diffnent headquarters of Generals and Colonels.

The Music from the Bands echoed and reeched across hill and Vale as cheerfully and gay as if there was none missing from the last Earthly roll-call.

But I am digressing—Having obtained My pass and money I Exchanged My blue pants for a pair of diffnent color and bidding farewell to my companions in camp, with a Sad heart was Soon on my Way to Culpeper C.H. Where I took the train for Washington and arrived about 2. o clock that night. Next Morning I proceeded to Genl Popes," Headquarters on 17th Street, oppisite the war Department, and obtained a pass to Fredericksburg. and going to 7th Street Wharf took the Steamer

Keyport (then in government Services) for Aquia Creek and on landing I found that there was no passengers permitted to go over to Fredericksburg till next day.

A Locomotive and train of flat cars Was waiting on the track to take over a lot of troops of Genl Burnsides command, and While they were getting on the train I got on with them Without the knowledge of the proper officer of the road. and Was Soon after landed at Falmouth Station about one mile this Side of the Rappahannock River. I walked over to the Town Where I found My wife, as Well as might be expected; They were all greatly Surprised to See Me. When they supposed Me to be at Culpeper County With Genl. King. I Remained at home about one Week, Enjoying My freedom With friends and aquaintances. the old rebel citizens Showing evident Marks of displeasure at My appearance among them. They regarding me in the light of a Spy or traitor to their cause. I had intended now to Stay at home and make a living and after a While, perhaps, to go North Some where, When My Wife Would possible be able to go With me,* as the Movements of both Armys (Union and Reble) were quite uncertain I did not know What minute the present force under Genl A. E. Burnside might be orderd away. The troops Were continually Moving to and fro and heavy fireing had been heard, for Several Days, in the direction of Culpeper C.H.

And a great many Soilders had crossed from Fredericksburg to the North Side of the river and and [sic] disapeared Soon after, Which gave rise Soon that they Yankee was falling back. My Wife and friends advised Me not to let the Yankees leave me behind if they did fall back, as they firmly beleived the rebels would take My life.

My Wife's Mother had not Spoken to her or me Since our Marrage and She had forbidden Annie to darken her door Way again or I Should have gone to Washington with My Wife and Settled down but as it Was my Wife was not in a condition to travel far Without and Elder female friend.* So Mrs Jackson and others of our friends advised me to leave at the Earliest opportunity for the Sake of Safety. and When My Wife Should be able She could come to Washington.

COMMENTS ON CHAPTER 10

Orders had Just been issued for the Discharge of all Servants Except hostlers and Cooks. This comment is interesting because it shows how the

Union forces used and dispensed with slaves during the war, as the bat-
tlefield situation changed, likely discharging personal servants during
times of movement and retaining only those necessary to feed and tend
soldiers and horses.

A Reward of $300.00 had been offered for my head in Fredericksburg.
Washington gives no indication as to who posted the reward or where
it was advertised.

*I had intended now to Stay at home and make a living and after a While,
perhaps, to go North Some where, When My Wife Would possible be able to
go With me.* The desire to see his wife explains why Washington would
return to Fredericksburg despite a $300 bounty, real or imagined, adver-
tised for his capture. As the following recollections show, he thoroughly
enjoyed gloating over his condition of freedom.

That Washington mentions his wife without going into much detail
is not unusual in nineteenth-century African American autobiography.
Frederick Douglass mentions his first wife, Anna Murray, only a few
times in his antebellum autobiographies, and like Washington he does not
detail the circumstances of their meeting, courtship, or inner feelings.

*My Wife was not in a condition to travel far Without and Elder female
friend.* The recollections provide no explanation for why Washington's
wife cannot travel, though the timing of their first son's birth later that
year indicates that Annie was pregnant. Leaving his wife in Fredericksburg, as Washington makes clear, was a wrenching decision to make.
Later, Washington was able to reunite with her in the nation's capital
after he found employment bottling liquor.

11

Finding Work

Sunday afternoon Augt. 31st 1862

About 4. clock. P.M. Our attention was called to a dark smoke over in Falmouth and going to the River Shore, we discoverd that the Union Troops Were burning their Bakery, which was very extensive and breaking up their camp in haste. With a sad heart I returned to tell My wife, the bad news, for I knew well what it meant that our troops were Evacuating Falmouth, I bid my wife good-by and hastened to the Headquarters of Col Kingsbury,* Provost Marshall of the Town to ascertain the facts in the case. I found Col Kingsbury in his office and Stepping up to him Saluted him and Said Colonel I heard Sir, that the Union troops are going to Evacuate the Town is it so Sir. What is it to you Son, go out of this office: "Said he." in a Stern commanding voice. bringing his clenched fist down on the table in front of him—I beg your pardon Colonel, "I Said" I am Genl King's Mess-Servant. Well What are you doing here

I Just came down on a Visit to My Wife Sir, and don't Want to be left behind if you all are going.

Well (in a Milder Voice now) if you Want to get away go right across the Bridge within 15 minutes

He gave me a pass and I was Soon across the wire Bridge I had not had time to go back home for any clothing or money and I had only 50 cents in my pocket—when I crossed the bridge I noticed shavings and Tar places at intervals on Several different piers With kegs of powder near by.

After crossing the Bridge I hastened to the Top of the Hill. At the East end of the Bridge, and looked back at the town that had given me birth and with a sad heart and full eyes thought of Some of the Joys I had felt within the limits—But now compelled to fly from it for my life, for daring to make my Escape to the Union army. and with a price fixed upon My head if caught, I could not help Weeping (though it was not manly) as I looked back, and thought of My poor young Wife, who could not fly With me—The Rebels was at that very minnit Swarming the Heights West of Fredericksburg.* and I know not, but they might take

Vengence on her as I had Escaped they could lock her up in Jail or any thing else and who would protect her.

My Solequey [Washington is perhaps substituting "soliloquy" for "reverie"] was interrupted by a tremendous Explosion that could be heard for Miles around, and Shook the Earth like an Earthquake. the Flame Shot upward hundreds of feet into the air—and as Suddenly all was Silent as death, But the Wire Bridge was gone to ruins and the rebels victorious Shout rang out over the Hights of Fredericksburg.

* * * [in original] Between 9 and 10 o clock that night I laid down in and out building at the Lacy Farm.* With the Union Army encamped all around me. When I awoke next Morning, a little after day light not a Soilder could be Seen any where about. The Whole of "Burnsides" Division had fallen back toward Aquia Creek on the Potomac River 15 miles distant. My case was a critical one now, indeed. A rain late in the Night had completely hid the track of the army, but I Soon Struck out for the railroad and after following it for Some time I left it and persued the road toward Bell-Plane Landing 9 miles distant. after walking for Some time I discovered the fresh tracks of Horses going the Same Way that I was, but Soon I could hear Voices. I Stoped and listened for I did not know Whether they were Rebel gorrillas or the Union army. I hid in the thick undergroth close by till I caught site of a blue coat. When My heart gave a great leap for Joy, I was Soon once More in the Union lines and about 2 o clock arrived at Aquia Creek Landing. I found the Soilders encamped for Miles around and Hundreds of Steamers and Transports of all discriptions awaiting to receive their living Cargoes, which was being shipped in all haste. When I got there the Mail Steamer Keyport was nearly ready to leave for Washington D.C.

I had Several old passes certifying that I was a Servant at Genl Kings Headquarters (but his headquarters was now up near Culpper Court-House) and consequently his passes was not respected. So the Sentinel guarding the Gang plank from the Wharf to the Steamer forbid me going aboard Without a pass from Gen. Burnside whose Headquarters Was near by. I Stood around a few minutes watching an opportunity When the Sentinel Stood reading another pass. I bounded across the Gang plank and concealed Myself for a while until the Steamer got off from the wharf. I then came out and arrived Safe at 6th Street Wharf in Washington D.C.* on the Night of September 1st 1862, in a hard rain. My Grandmother, Aunt and her 4 children all Slept on 14th St that Night and next morning walked to Georgetown Where we had friends My Grandmother aunt and the children Soon found Some place to Stay, and I obtained board at Mrs. Boons at $2.50 per Week. My next object Was to obtain Work in order that I Might pay my board and get a change of clothing for I Was Sadly in need of them—I had no trade then and knew not what to do. But Soon Learned to turn My hand to Most any thing light. there was a plenty of heavy work. Such [as] loading and unloading Vessels and Steamers but that was mostly to heavy for me, as I was not very strong but finnally obtained a place Bottling Liquor for Dodge & c at $1.25 per day which lasted for Some time.

COMMENTS ON CHAPTER 11

I bid my wife good-by and hastened to the Headquarters of Col Kingsbury. Colonel Walter Kingsbury, as Washington notes, was the Union provost marshal in Fredericksburg. On 13 August, in retaliation for previous imprisonment of Unionists by Confederate authorities, he had arrested nineteen Fredericksburg civilians, including Mayor Montgomery Slaughter, and ordered them to appear before him to show cause why they should not be confined to prison.[1]

The Rebels was at that very minnit Swarming the Heights West of Fredericksburg. The Union army decided to evacuate Falmouth sometime before September. In an entry for 5 September, Betty Maury expresses jubilation that the Yankees are evacuating and notes that on Monday morning, "Mr. White and several others went to see if they could recover some of 'their negroes.'"[2] In a diary entry of 31 August, Elizabeth Maxwell Wynne, a 16-year-old girl with very pro-Confederate sympathies, described the events this way: "Union men packed up & left . . . Contrabands tied up bundles, put them on their heads, took their little ones in their arms & by the hand and started for the depot . . . or any where, so as to get away before the town was shelled. Ladies, young & old, children of both sexes & old men collected on the streets to see the Yankees depart . . . When the villains crossed over the river, & set the bridges on fire, we all collected at Mr. Knox' corner to witness their distruction . . . it was very beautiful indeed."[3]

I laid down in and out building at the Lacy Farm. The Lacys had farms at Chatham, Greenwood, and Ellwood. They supported the Confederacy. Only with the Union army all around him would Washington have been safe.

I then came out and arrived Safe at 6th Street Wharf in Washington D.C. Washington lived a long life after the war. A remarkable witness to some pivotal events in American history, he led an unobtrusive life in the nation's capital and focused his energies on earning a living and being a dedicated husband and father. His wife Annie joined him in Washington, D.C., and there they had a son, William, in 1862. John worked as a house painter in the District of Columbia, and Annie earned income as a dressmaker. By 1880, they had five sons; William worked as a scourer, while James, John, Charles, and the youngest, Benjamin, attended school. Benjamin was teaching high school by the turn of the twentieth century. He and William were living with their parents in the District of Columbia at the time of the 1900 census, which also indicates that John and Annie had been married thirty-eight years. By 1910, John and Annie had retired, and Benjamin was taking care of his elderly parents. William had moved to Massachusetts and was earning a living as a shipper in a shoe store in Boston. He had married and had a son of his own. Washington may have joined his eldest son in Boston, for he died in Massachusetts in 1918 at the age of eighty.[4] A life begun in slavery ended during World War I. Unfortunately, we have no indications of how Washington dealt with the virulent racism of the Jim Crow period. By 1920, Annie was living in Chicago keeping house for William, who was working in a real estate office, and her daughter-in-law Louise, a stenographer. Annie helped look after her teenaged grandson, Earle.[5]

APPENDIX

John Washington's Geography

In chapter 8 of "Memorys of the Past," Washington includes a hand-drawn map of Fredericksburg, reproduced on the following page. Upon casual examination, the unusual map appears to be little more than a crude drawing of the Fredericksburg area. Done in pencil with relative locations and some of the numbered spots impossible to make out, the map seems to be little more than doodles on the paper. I recall my first reaction to it as dismissive, something not worthy of much attention in an otherwise engrossing story. But upon more thoughtful reflection, the "Vicinity of Fredericksburg Va" map takes on a deeper meaning within the broader context of Washington's narrative. Scrutinized closely, his compass points on the Rappahannock River clearly fix the coordinates of freedom—places where his life intersected with events, people, or moments when the thoughts of liberty touched his memory. Every point can be connected to a map point that relates to emancipation or the rewards of freedom in some way: the Railroad Bridge, burned by retreating Rebel armies; Coalters Bridge, where the town council reluctantly surrendered Fredericksburg to the Union army; the mills, where as a boy Washington played hooky on Sunday afternoons when he was supposed to be in church; the tobacco factory, where freedom meant the singing of slaves and the warmth of community; Myre's Heights, which represented one of the bloodiest battles for freedom during the entire Civil War; the Shakespeare House, where Washington celebrated freedom's army in the forms of glistening bayonets (its location appears in large, bold print as "UNION CAMP" on his map); the "Forrest," where he found brief respite from the "Old Mistress"; the Pontoon Bridge, built by the Yankee armies before they successfully stormed the town; and finally, "Where I crossed the river," Washington's final journey into freedom. Although we cannot be sure that the map was a deliberate attempt to mark the boundaries of slavery and freedom, it is far more than just coincidental that every location on it is a freedom coordinate in "Memorys of the Past."

where Mrs Mazene lived (the proprietors wife) and delivered the keys to her.

1. Railroad Bridge
2. Island
3. Coalters Bridge
4. Woolen mills
5. Basin
6. Knoxs mill
7. Ficklins mill
8. Ficklins Heights
9. Railroad Depot
10. Tobbacco Factory
11. Myers Heights
12. Sheakespeare House
13. Ferry Wharf
14. Pontoon Bridge
15. Forrest
16. Where I crossed the River

Vicinity of Fredericksburg Va.

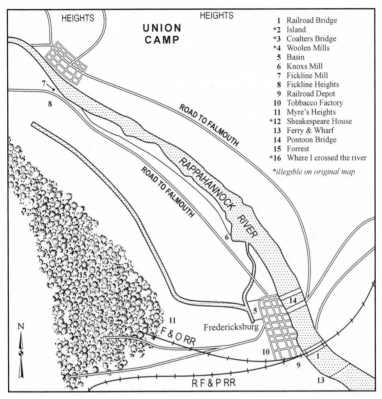

Washington's map of Fredericksburg as it appeared in "Memorys of the Past" (*left*) and redrawn (*above*). Redrawn by Mary Lee Eggart.

NOTES

Introduction: Fredericksburg in 1838

1. Workers of the Writers' Program of the Work Projects Administration in the State of Virginia, comp., *Virginia: A Guide to the Old Dominion* (Richmond: Virginia State Library and Archives, 1992), 10, hereafter cited as WPA *Guide*.

2. Ibid.

3. Emily J. Salmon and Edward D. C. Campbell, Jr., eds., *The Hornbook of Virginia History: A Ready-Reference Guide to the Old Dominion's People, Places, and Past*, 4th ed. (Richmond: Library of Virginia, 1994), 170, 191. See also S. J. Quinn, *The History of the City of Fredericksburg, Virginia* (Richmond: Heritage Press, 1908), 37.

4. *Virginia Herald*, 3 February and 4 August 1816, 9 September 1840. On the Atlantic as connecting West African rivers to New World river traffic, see John Thornton, *Africa and Africans in the Making of the Atlantic World, 1400–1680* (Cambridge: Cambridge University Press, 1992).

5. *Virginia Herald*, 3 February 1816.

6. Noel G. Harrison, *Fredericksburg Civil War Sites*, vol. 2, *December 1862–April 1865* (Lynchburg, Va.: H. E. Howard, 1995), 241–44.

7. There do not seem to be any data pertaining to Fredericksburg as a subset of the regional trade. The anecdotal evidence to follow should both highlight the "big" picture of forced migration and give a sense of what the Fredericksburg market was like.

8. Quinn, *The History of the City of Fredericksburg*, 168, photograph following 296; Ruth Coder Fitzgerald, *A Different Story: A Black History of Fredericksburg, Stafford, and Spotsylvania, Virginia* (Greensboro, N.C.: Unicorn, 1979), 5.

9. Ethan Allen Andrews, *Slavery and the Domestic Slave-Trade in the United States* (Boston: Light and Stearns, 1836), 165.

10. Ibid., 168.

11. Michael Tadman, *Speculators and Slaves: Masters, Traders, and Slaves in the Old South* (Madison: University of Wisconsin Press, 1989), 169.

12. Andrews, *Slavery and the Domestic Slave-Trade*, 165.

13. Steven Deyle, "The Domestic Slave Trade in America: The Lifeblood of the Southern Slave System," in *The Chattel Principle: Internal Slave Trades in the Americas*, ed. Walter Johnson (New Haven: Yale University Press, 2004), 93. See also Deyle, *Carry Me Back: The Domestic Slave Trade in American Life* (New York: Oxford University Press, 2005), appendixes A and B; Tadman, *Speculators and Slaves*, ch. 2.

14. Andrews, *Slavery and the Domestic Slave-Trade*, 164–65; Charles L. Perdue, Jr., Thomas E. Barden, and Robert K. Phillips, eds., *Weevils in the Wheat: Interviews with Virginia Ex-Slaves* (Charlottesville: University Press of Virginia, 1976), 33; Andrews, *Slavery and the Domestic Slave-Trade*, 166.

15. WPA *Guide*, 218. My understanding of ritual display in colonial and Revolutionary Virginia has been shaped by Rhys Isaac, *The Transformation of Virginia, 1740–1790* (Chapel Hill: University of North Carolina Press, 1982). The ethnography of social relations in late-eighteenth-century Virginia is developed admirably in Isaac's chapter entitled "A Discourse on the Method: Action, Structure, and Meaning," 323–60. On the place of honor in southern culture, see Bertram Wyatt-Brown, *Southern Honor: Ethics and Behavior in the Old South* (New York: Oxford University Press, 1982); and Edward L. Ayers, *Vengeance and Justice: Crime and Punishment in the Nineteenth-Century American South* (New York: Oxford University Press, 1984).

16. Stephen V. Ash, *Middle Tennessee Society Transformed, 1860–1870: War and Peace in the Upper South* (Baton Rouge: Louisiana State University Press, 1988), 9–10.

17. Crandall Shifflett, "In the Eye of the Storm: The Civil War in Fredericksburg, Virginia," paper presented at the 1993 annual meeting, Organization of American Historians, Anaheim, California. See also W. A. Blair, "Barbarians at Fredericksburg's Gate: The Impact of the Union Army on Civilians," in *The Fredericksburg Campaign: Decision on the Rappahannock*, ed. Gary W. Gallagher (Chapel Hill: University of North Carolina Press, 1995), 145; Elizabeth Getz, "'Take a Good Ready and Start Monday Morning': Abraham Lincoln in Fredericksburg, May 1862," *Journal of Fredericksburg History* 4 (1999): 23.

18. Frederick Law Olmstead, *A Journey in the Seaboard Slave States, with Remarks on their Economy* (New York: Dix and Edwards, 1856), 20–21; see also WPA *Guide*, 217–18.

19. John d'Entremont, *Southern Emancipator: Moncure Conway, the American Years, 1832–1865* (New York: Oxford University Press, 1987), xii.

20. Launcelot Minor Blackford, *Mine Eyes Have Seen the Glory: The Story of a Virginia Lady, Mary Berkeley Minor Blackford, 1802–1896, Who Taught Her Sons to Hate Slavery and to Love the Union* (Cambridge, Mass.: Harvard University Press, 1954); Blair, "Barbarians at Fredericksburg's Gate," 148.

21. Blair, "Barbarians at Fredericksburg's Gate," 148.

22. Noah Davis, *A Narrative of the Life of Rev. Noah Davis, a Colored Man, Written by Himself, at the Age of Fifty-Four* (Baltimore: John F. Weishampel, Jr., 1859), 2; Fitzgerald, *A Different Story*, 44.

23. Davis, *Narrative*, 15.

24. Petition to the General Assembly, 18 March 1838, Virginia State Library and Archives, Richmond, Virginia, as reproduced in David Hackett Fischer and James C. Kelly, *Away, I'm Bound Away: Virginia and the Westward Movement* (Richmond: Virginia Historical Society, 1993), 244; Luther Porter Jackson, *Free Negro Labor and Property Holding in Virginia, 1830–1860* (New York: D. Appleton-Century Co., 1942).

25. Nell Irvin Painter, "Representing Truth: Sojourner Truth's Knowing and Becoming Known," *Journal of American History* 81, no. 2 (1994): 466–67.

1. Childhood

1. U.S. Federal Census, 1860: Place: Fredericksburg, Spotsylvania, Virginia; Roll: M653_1380; Page: 319; Image: 321 (http://content.ancestry.com/iexec/?htx=List&dbid =7667&offerid=0%3a7858%3a0); Noel G. Harrison, *Fredericksburg Civil War Sites*, vol.

1, *April 1861–November 1862* (M. E. Howard, Inc., 1995), 120. Washington's "Memorys" does not refer to any other slaves in her household.

2. Richard C. Wade, *Slavery in the Cities: The South, 1820–1860* (New York: Oxford University Press, 1964). The situation varied greatly from city to city. See, for example, David R. Goldfield, *Urban Growth in the Age of Sectionalism: Virginia, 1847–1861* (Baton Rouge: Louisiana State University Press, 1977), and John W. Blassingame, *Black New Orleans, 1860–1880* (Chicago: University of Chicago Press, 1973).

3. Nor was such a person found in Vee Dove, *Madison County Homes: A Collection of Pre–Civil War Homes and Family Heritages* (Kingsport, Tenn.: Kingsport Press, 1975).

4. Fischer and Kelly, *Away, I'm Bound Away*, 243 (first quotation); *The Code of Virginia, Including Legislation to the Year 1860*, 2nd ed. (Richmond, 1860), 810–11 (second and third quotations). See Painter, "Representing Truth," 465.

5. Washington's photograph reveals a very light-skinned, round-faced, balding man probably in his fifties, dressed in coat and tie with a moustache and goatee, upturned face, and a kind, inquisitive look. The photograph appeared in a *New York Times* article (14 June 2004) which unwittingly reported that historian David Blight had suddenly "discovered" the John Washington diary. Unfortunately, the Massachusetts Historical Society, identified in the article as the repository, and The Strothman Agency, LLC, refused requests to use the photograph.

6. Data are taken from the Seventh U.S. Census, 1850: Historical Census Browser, Geospatial and Statistical Data Center, University of Virginia, http://fisher.lib.virginia .edu/collections/stats/histcensus/index.html (accessed 25 October 2006).

7. John W. Blassingame, *The Slave Community: Plantation Life in the Antebellum South* (New York: Oxford University Press, 1972); Lawrence W. Levine, *Black Culture and Black Consciousness: Afro-American Folk Thought from Slavery to Freedom* (New York: Oxford University Press, 1977).

8. Higginson is quoted in Reid Mitchell, *The Vacant Chair: The Northern Soldier Leaves Home* (New York: Oxford University Press, 1993), 61. According to the opposite view, "The best preventive of theft is plenty of pork"; see Ulrich B. Phillips, *American Negro Slavery: A Survey of the Supply, Employment, and Control of Negro Labor as Determined by the Plantation Regime* (Baton Rouge: Louisiana State University Press, 1966), 276. For slave views, see Perdue, Barden, and Phillips, eds., *Weevils in the Wheat*. The place of physical conditions in the hierarchy of slave values was examined in a comparative context in Eugene D. Genovese, "The Treatment of Slaves in Different Countries: Problems in the Application of the Comparative Method," in *Slavery in the New World: A Reader in Comparative History*, edited by Laura Foner and Eugene D. Genovese (Englewood Cliffs, N.J.: Prentice-Hall, 1969), 202–03, and Eugene D. Genovese, *Roll, Jordan, Roll: The World the Slaves Made* (New York: Pantheon, 1974). Former slaves recalled whippings more memorable than rations of food and clothing in Paul D. Escott, *Slavery Remembered: A Record of Twentieth-Century Slave Narratives* (Chapel Hill: University of North Carolina Press, 1979).

9. Orlando Patterson, *Slavery and Social Death: A Comparative Study* (Cambridge, Mass.: Harvard University Press, 1982), 207.

10. See Wayne K. Durrill, "Routine of Seasons: Labour Regimes and Social Ritual

in an Antebellum Plantation Community," *Slavery and Abolition* 16 no. 2 (August 1995): 161–87. The author examines a county in northeastern North Carolina that produced corn as a cash crop, but his findings hold for the region as a whole.

11. Frederick Douglass, *Narrative of the Life of Frederick Douglass, an American Slave, Written by Himself* (Boston: Published at the Anti-Slavery Office, 1845), 74. http://docsouth .unc.edu/neh/douglass/douglass.html (accessed 25 October 2006).

12. Frederick Douglass, *My Bondage and My Freedom* (New York: Miller, Orton & Mulligan, 1855), 253. http://docsouth.unc.edu/neh/douglass55/douglass55.html (accessed 26 October 2006).

13. For a study of corn-shucking ceremonies where white masters hosted slaves and encouraged them to perform exuberant displays of dancing and reverie, see Roger D. Abrahams, *Singing the Master: The Emergence of African American Culture in the Plantation South* (New York: Pantheon, 1992).

14. Douglass, *My Bondage and My Freedom,* 252. http://docsouth.unc.edu/neh/douglass55/ douglass55.html (accessed 27 October 2006).

2. Slavery

1. Tadman, *Speculators and Slaves,* 12; Willie Lee Rose, *A Documentary History of Slavery in North America* (New York: Oxford University Press, 1976); Patterson, *Slavery and Social Death;* Donald B. Dodd, comp., *Historical Statistics of the States of the United States: Two Centuries of the Census, 1790–1990* (Westport, Conn.: Greenwood Press, 1993), 93; John B. Duff and Peter M. Mitchell, eds., *The Nat Turner Rebellion: The Historical Event and the Modern Controversy* (New York: Harper & Row, 1971).

2. Harrison, *Civil War Sites,* vol. 1, 120. The building survived the battles of Fredericksburg with only minor damage.

3. See Ben Sellers, "John Washington, Former Fredericksburg Slave, Gains Fame Through His Memoirs," *Free Lance-Star* (Fredericksburg, Va.), 23 February 2006; Shiloh Baptist Church website: http://www.shiloholdsite.org/members1854.htm (accessed 26 October 2006).

4. Harrison, *Civil War Sites,* vol. 2, 198.

5. Blassingame, *The Slave Community,* ch. 2. On the origins and meaning of the "shout" dance, see Sterling Stuckey, *Slave Culture: Nationalist Theory and the Foundations of Black America* (New York: Oxford University Press, 1987), introduction, 3–97. Slave spirituals and secular songs are treated extensively in Levine, *Black Culture and Black Consciousness.* On slave religion, see also Genovese, *Roll, Jordan, Roll;* and Albert J. Raboteau, *Slave Religion: The "Invisible Institution" in the Antebellum South* (New York: Oxford University Press, 1978).

5. Growing Up

1. Carrol H. Quenzel, *The History and Background of St. George's Episcopal Church, Fredericksburg, Virginia* (Richmond: Privately printed, 1951); Harrison, *Civil War Sites,* vol. 2, 192–96.

2. On the "Sambo" personality type, see Stanley M. Elkins, *Slavery: A Problem in American Institutional and Intellectual Life*, 2nd ed. (Chicago: University of Chicago Press, 1968). The historiography of slavery is too vast to summarize here, but examples of different views include Herbert Aptheker, *Negro Slave Revolts in the United States, 1526–1860* (New York: International Publishers, 1939); and Blassingame, *The Slave Community.* For a survey of the slavery literature, see Peter J. Parish, *Slavery: History and Historians* (New York: Harper & Row, 1989), and Lawrence B. Goodheart, Richard D. Brown, and Stephen G. Rabe, eds., *Slavery in American Society*, 3rd ed. (Lexington, Mass.: D.C. Heath and Co., 1993). On the antecedents and causes of slave revolts in a comparative context, see Eugene Genovese, *From Rebellion to Revolution: Afro-American Slave Revolts in the Making of the Modern World* (Baton Rouge: Louisiana State University Press, 1979).

3. David J. Rothman, *The Discovery of the Asylum: Social Order and Disorder in the New Republic* (Boston: Little, Brown, 1971).

4. Douglas Young, "A Brief History of the Staunton and James River Turnpike" (Charlottesville: Virginia Highway & Transportation Research Council), 1975 [revised 2003]), 7–9. http://www.virginiadot.org/vtrc/main/online_reports/pdf/75-r59.pdf (accessed 26 October 2006).

6. Finding a Wife

1. Quinn, *The History of the City of Fredericksburg*, 74, 77–78.

2. Andrew Witmer, "Race, Religion, and Rebellion: Black and White Baptists in Albemarle County, Virginia, during the Civil War," in *Crucible of the Civil War: Virginia from Secession to Commemoration*, ed. Edward L. Ayers, Gary W. Gallagher, and Andrew J. Torget (Charlottesville: University of Virginia Press, 2006). John Thornton has shown revelation theology to be a part of Afro-Atlantic religion that inspired Africans during and after the slave trade. The belief in continuous revelation would explain how Washington's conversion experience and later manifestations of God acting in the world resonated with him. See Thornton, *Africa and Africans in the Making of the Atlantic World*, ch. 9.

3. It is unclear whether this in fact was the factory where Washington worked, although no other tobacco factory is listed in Harrison, *Civil War Sites,* vol. 1, 76–80. No reference to Alexander and Gibbs could be found, and this list of slaves does not include someone of Washington's age, although the 20-year-old would have been close.

4. Alexander Mackay, *The Western World; or, Travels in the United States in 1846–47: Exhibiting Them in Their Latest Development, Social, Political and Industrial, Including a Chapter on California,* vol. I (Philadelphia: Lea & Blanchard, 1849), 285.

5. See Alan Bruce Bromberg, "Slavery in the Virginia Tobacco Factories, 1800–1860" (M.A. thesis, University of Virginia, 1968).

6. Leni Sorensen, "Absconded: Fugitive Slaves in the Daybook of the Richmond Police Guard" (Ph.D. dissertation, College of William and Mary, 2005), 38–66.

7. The figure of $120–$125 per year comes from the contemporary investigation of Robert Russell, *North America, Its Agriculture and Climate: Containing Observations on the Agriculture and Climate of Canada, the United States, and the Island of Cuba* (Edinburgh: Adam and Charles Black, 1857), 151.

8. Ibid., 17.

9. Bryant quoted in Workers of the Writers' Program of the Work Projects Administration in the State of Virginia, comp., *The Negro in Virginia* (Winston-Salem: John F. Blair, 1994), 59.

10. Ibid.

7. The War Comes

1. Harrison, *Civil War Sites,* vol. 1, 126, 127.

2. Ibid., 128.

3. d'Entremont, *Southern Emancipator,* 21.

4. Louis S. Gerteis, *From Contraband to Freedman: Federal Policy Toward Southern Blacks, 1861–1865* (Westport, Conn.: Greenwood Press, 1973).

5. See George C. Rable, *Fredericksburg! Fredericksburg!* (Chapel Hill: University of North Carolina Press, 2002).

6. U.S. Federal Census, 1850: Place: Eastern District, Spotsylvania, Virginia; Roll: M432_977; Page: 422; Image: 360 (http://content.ancestry.com/iexec/?htx=List&dbid =8054&offerid=0%3a7858%3a0 [accessed 2 November 2006]); U.S. Federal Census, 1870: Place: Fredericksburg, Spotsylvania, Virginia; Roll: M593_1679; Page: 369; Image: 740 (http://content.ancestry.com/iexec/?htx=List&dbid=7163&offerid=0%3a7858 %3a0 [accessed 2 November 2006]); Robert K. Krick, *30th Virginia Infantry* (Lynchburg, Va.: H. E. Howard, 1983), 114; Civil War Service Records, Box: 382; Extraction: 43; Record: 3825 (http://www.ancestry.com/search/db.aspx?dbid=4284 [accessed 28 October 2006]); U.S. Federal Census, 1860: Place: Fredericksburg, Spotsylvania, Virginia; Roll: M653_1380; Page: 294; Image: 296 (http://content.ancestry.com/iexec/ ?htx=List&dbid=7667&offerid=0%3a7858%3a0 [accessed 29 October 2006]).

7. Krick, *30th Virginia,* 34–35, 118; quotation appears on p. 34.

8. *Richmond Daily Dispatch,* 19 April 1862. http://dlxs.richmond.edu/d/ddr/ (accessed 9 November 2006).

8. First Night of Freedom

1. *The Journal of Jane Howison Beale of Fredericksburg, Virginia, 1850–1862* (Fredericksburg, Va.: Historic Fredericksburg, 1979), 37. Beale was born in Fredericksburg in 1815, one of twelve children of Samuel and Helen Moore Howison. The family home was St. James, an eighteenth-century house on Charles Street. The Howisons belonged to the Fredericksburg Presbyterian Church. At nineteen, Jane married William Churchill Beale, and they lived in a brick house in Falmouth near the Rappahannock River. William Beale was a successful merchant-miller who died in 1850. After his death, Jane began to keep a diary, and she founded a school for girls located in her backyard and supplemented her income by taking in boarders.

2. Diary of Betty Herndon Maury, Central Rappahannock Regional Library, Virginiana Collection, Fredericksburg, 49. Maury was the daughter of a famous geographer, Matthew Fontaine Maury, whose observations on wind and ocean currents earned him

the distinction "Pathfinder of the Seas." His bust is on display at the state capitol in Richmond. When the war started, he resigned his federal position and came home from Washington, D.C., to head harbor and river defenses for the Confederacy. A dedicated partisan, he invented the "electric torpedo" and traveled to England to acquire materials for its production.

3. Minutes of the City Council, Central Rappahannock Regional Library, 29–35.

4. Maury Diary, 52.

5. Individual perceptions from three generations of women in the Maury family reveal how the trope of patriarchy developed and matured, as slavery fixed itself on antebellum Virginia between 1800 and the Civil War. Betty's mother, for example, said her generation never felt the evils of the Union and she regretted that future generations would never know the advantages of a lifetime of independence as a southern nation. Her daughter Betty responded that the evils would have been felt sooner or later, and that her generation was fighting for "the good of posterity, and we may prevent a servile war." Betty's mother made almost no reference to slavery, whereas Betty made it clear that the slaves must be held at all costs. Ultimately Betty's daughter, Nannie Belle, revealed how well the third generation had learned the lessons of a patriarchal society. As Betty reports it, Nannie Belle and her friend Sally Woolfolk were "playing ladies." Sally dressed herself using a mosquito net for a shawl and came "to call" on Nannie Belle. Sally: "Good Morning, Maam, how are you today?" Nannie Belle: "I don't feel very well this morning, all my niggers have run away and left me." Ibid., 45, 66. One study of married men's wills of estate for the period 1890–1905 found that although the war did not bring a new era of opportunities for Fredericksburg women or radically change relations between the sexes, it did diminish antebellum patriarchy. Wills of Civil War–era husbands reveal more generosity in the treatment of their wives, reflecting a minor shift in the power relations inside the family. See Edward J. Harcourt, "The Civil War and Social Change: White Women in Fredericksburg, Virginia" (master's thesis, University of Richmond, 1997).

6. *New York Herald,* 4 April 1862; James M. McPherson, ed., *Encyclopedia of Civil War Biographies,* vol. 1 (Armonk, N.Y.: Sharpe Reference, 2000), 40–41.

7. Maury Diary, 40.

8. David S. Heidler and Jeanne T. Heidler, *Encyclopedia of the American Civil War: A Political, Social, and Military History* (Santa Barbara, Calif.: ABC-CLIO, 2000), vol. 1, 147–48, vol. 2, 774.

9. Unsigned letter from the sister of Samuel S. Brooke to Sam and Mr. Bruce, 17 April 1862, in Samuel S. Brooke Papers, Virginia Military Institute Archives, MS 221. http://www.vmi.edu/ARCHIVES/Manuscripts/ms022101.html (accessed 28 October 2006).

10. Harrison, *Civil War Sites,* vol. 2, 11.

11. McPherson, ed., *Encyclopedia of Civil War Biographies,* vol. 1, 40–41; Heidler and Heidler, *Encyclopedia of the American Civil War,* vol. 1, 147–48.

12. Gordon W. Shelton, "Fredericksburg Water Power, 1822–1922," in folder entitled "Rappahannock Water Power," Central Rappahannock Regional Library.

13. Records of the G.A.O., Records of the Third Auditor's Office, Southern Claims Commission Case Files, 1871–1880. Virginia: Shenandoah to Spotsylvania Counties. Record Group 217, Boxes 397–98, Washington, D.C.: National Archives and Records Ad-

ministration (hereafter SCC Records); Fitzgerald, *A Different Story,* 20–21. Ficklin was awarded $8,202 from a claim of $23,583, despite the difficulty of proving Union allegiance in the South. A total of 22,298 claims were filed for damages over $60 million, but only 7,092 claims were allowed for a total of about $4.5 million. See Frank Wysor Klingberg, *The Southern Claims Commission* (Millwood, N.Y.: Kraus Reprint, 1980), iv–v. In 1994, I gave a lecture for the Historic Fredericksburg Foundation entitled "Unionism in Fredericksburg," in which I presented evidence of Ficklin's wartime sympathies, much to the astonishment of his Belmont home curators, who learned of Ficklin's unionism for the first time. The SCC Records document an unexpected level of unionism in Civil War Fredericksburg, as annotations in this book demonstrate. According to the Personal Property Tax Records, Stafford County, 1867, Ficklin had 2 horses, 1 cow, 2 hogs, 1 wagon, 3 watches, 1 clock, 1 piano, and furniture worth $1,000. He received $1,761 in annual rent on the toll bridge that he controlled between Falmouth and Fredericksburg. I am indebted to Richard Lowe, University of North Texas, for this personal property tax record from Stafford County. The 1860 Census of Population shows Ficklin owning real estate estimated to be worth $100,000 and personal property of $300,000. U.S. Census, Stafford County, Roll 1375, Stafford Court House, p.1.

14. Civil War Service Records, Box: 551; Extraction: 79; Record: 2191. http://www .ancestry.com/search/db.aspx?dbid=4284 (accessed 29 October 2006).

15. U.S. Census, 1870: Place: Northampton County, Fulton, New York; Roll: M593_938; Page: 275; Image: 554. http://content.ancestry.com/iexec/?htx=List&dbid=7163&offerid =0%3a7858%3a0 (accessed 29 October 2006).

16. Unsigned letter from the sister of Samuel S. Brooke to Sam and Mr. Bruce, 17 April 1862, in Brooke Papers, VMI Archives, MS 221. http://www.vmi.edu/ARCHIVES/ Manuscripts/ms022101.html (accessed 28 October 2006).

17. David J. Eicher, *The Longest Night: A Military History of the Civil War* (New York: Simon & Schuster, 2001), 230.

18. William R. Ray, entry for 15 April 1862, in *Four Years with the Iron Brigade: The Civil War Journals of William R. Ray, Co. F., Seventh Wisconsin Infantry,* ed. Lance J. Herdegen and Sherry Murphy (Cambridge, Mass.: Da Capo Press, 2002), 79.

19. Marsena Rudolph Patrick, *Inside Lincoln's Army: The Diary of Marsena Rudolph Patrick, Provost Marshall General, Army of the Potomac,* ed. David S. Sparks (New York: Thomas Yoseloff, 1964), 70.

20. *Richmond Daily Dispatch,* 19 December 1862, http://dlxs.richmond.edu/d/ddr/ (accessed 9 November 2006); "Report of Col. Samuel K. Zook, Fifty-seventh New York Infantry . . . Battle of Fredericksburg, Va.," *The War of the Rebellion: A Compilation of the Official Records of the Union and Confederate Armies,* (Washington, D.C.: U.S. War Department, 1880–1901, ser. I, vol. 21 [S# 31], http://www.civilwarhome.com/zookfredericks burg.htm (accessed 9 November 2006); "Report of Capt. Samuel T. Cushing, Commissary of Subsistence . . . —The Chancellorsville Campaign," *Official Records,* ser. I, vol. XXV/1 [S# 39], http://www.civilwarhome.com/cushingchancellorsvilleor.htm (accessed 9 November 2006).

21. U.S. Federal Census, 1860: Place: Watertown Ward 7, Jefferson, Wisconsin; Roll: M653_1413; Page: 784; Image: 789 (http://content.ancestry.com/iexec/?htx=List

&dbid=7667&offerid=0%3a7858%3a0 [accessed 9 November 2006]); U.S. Federal Census, 1870: Place: Ellsworth, Pierce, Wisconsin; Roll: M593_1731; Page: 292; Image: 585 (http://content.ancestry.com/iexec/?htx=List&dbid=7163&offerid=0%3a7858%3a0 [accessed 9 November 2006]); American Civil War Soldiers database http://www.ancestry.com/search/rectype/military/cwrd/main.aspx (accessed 9 November 2006). This is probably not the man Washington encountered, and no other Captain Wood could be located in census records or any other record. The Wood whom Washington describes has the assuredness of a mature man and an able military officer, and does not sound like a boy who has been promoted on the field.

22. Ezra J. Warner, *Generals in Blue: Lives of the Union Commanders* (Baton Rouge: Louisiana State University Press, 1964), 269–70, quote on 270; William Frayne Amann, *Personnel of the Civil War*, vol. 2, *The Union Armies* (New York: Thomas Yoseloff, 1961), 242.

23. U.S. Federal Census, 1860: Place: Appleton Ward 3, Outagamie, Wisconsin; Roll: M653_1424; Page: 373; Image: 379 (accessed 4 November 2006).

24. U.S. Federal Census, 1870: Place: Chicago Ward 7, Cook, Illinois; Roll: M593_202; Page: 33; Image: 66 (http://content.ancestry.com/iexec/?htx=List&dbid=7163&offerid=0%3a7858%3a0 (accessed 4 November 2006); for the history of the Sixth Wisconsin: http://www.2manitowoc.com/cvwrinf1.html (accessed 4 November 4 2006); Civil War Service Records, Box: 559; Extraction: 17; Record: 2856, http://www.ancestry.com/search/db.aspx?dbid=4284 (accessed 4 November 2006).

25. Quinn, *The History of the City of Fredericksburg*, 76–77.

9. On the Move with the Union Army

1. Hillman Allyn Hall, *History of the Sixth New York Cavalry (Second Ira Harris Guard) Second Brigade—First Division—Cavalry Corps, Army of the Potomac, 1861–1865* (Worcester, Mass.: Blanchard Press, 1908), 16, 38.

2. Stewart Sifakis, *Who Was Who in the Civil War* (New York: Facts on File, 1988); James A. Ramage, *Gray Ghost: The Life of Col. John Singleton Mosby* (Lexington: University Press of Kentucky, 1999).

3. Harrison, *Civil War Sites*, vol. 1, 121.

11. Finding Work

1. Harrison, *Civil War Sites*, vol. 1, 121.

2. Maury Diary, 68.

3. Diary of Elizabeth Maxwell Wynne, 20 May 1862, MSS 1W9927, Virginia Historical Society.

4. Some of the details of Washington's later life after "Memorys" have been pieced together from records of the federal census. Unfortunately, the Massachusetts Historical Society has refused to release any of its material on Washington except to the *New York Times*, a literary agent, and historian David Blight.

5. U.S. Federal Census, 1880: Place: Washington, District of Columbia; Roll: T9_123; Family History Film: 1254123; Page: 47.4000; Enumeration District: 45; Image: 0096

(http://content.ancestry.com/iexec/?htx=List&dbid=6742&offerid=0%3a7858%3a0 [accessed 9 November 2006]); U.S. Federal Census, 1900: Place: Boston Ward 12, Suffolk, Mass.; Roll: T623 681; Page: 9A; Enumeration District: 1326 (http://content.ancestry.com/iexec/?htx=List&dbid=7602&offerid=0%3a7858%3a0 [accessed 9 November 2006]); U.S. Federal Census, 1910: Place: Precinct 8, Washington, District of Columbia; Roll: T624_153; Page: 8B; Enumeration District: 154; Image: 498 (http://content.ancestry.com/iexec/?htx=List&dbid=7884&offerid=0%3a7858%3a0 [accessed 9 November 2006]); U.S. Federal Census, 1920: Place: Chicago Ward 3, Cook (Chicago), Ill.; Roll: T625_312; Page: 2B; Enumeration District: 137; Image: 903 (http://content.ancestry.com/iexec/?htx=List&dbid=6061&offerid=0%3a7858%3a0 [accessed 9 November 2006]).

BIBLIOGRAPHY

Manuscripts, Diaries, and Government Records

Civil War Service Records, United States National Archives. Database on-line. Provo, Utah: The Generations Network, Inc., 1999. http://www.ancestry .com/search/db.aspx?dbid=4284.

The Code of Virginia, Including Legislation to the Year 1860. 2nd ed. Richmond: Ritchie, Dunnavent and Co., 1860.

Credit ledgers, 1840–1895, R. G. Dunn and Co. Collection. Baker Library, Harvard Business School.

Diary of Elizabeth Maxwell Wynne. MSS 1W9927, Virginia Historical Society.

Files and records in the Central Rappahannock Regional Library, Virginiana Collection, Fredericksburg, Virginia.

"Auctions, Hotels, Taverns."

Fredericksburg Heads of Household, 1860 and 1870.

Fredericksburg Slave Owners, 1860.

Free Negroes, Fredericksburg, 1850–1862.

Journal of Jane Howison Beale.

"Journal of Jason Clifton Grant."

"Journal of Lizzie Alsop."

"Life of Joseph F. Walker."

"Lizzie Van Wart Diary, 1900."

Minutes of the City Council, 1861–1865.

Shelton, Gordon W. "Fredericksburg Water Power, 1822–1922," in folder entitled "Rappahannock Water Power."

Spotsylvania County Slave Owners, 1860.

"Katherine Couse Civil War Letter." MS 10441, Special Collections, Alderman Library, University of Virginia.

Letter in Samuel S. Brooke Papers. MS 221, Virginia Military Institute Archives. http://www.vmi.edu/ARCHIVES/Manuscripts/ms022101.html.

Personal Property Tax Records, Stafford County, 1867.

Population Schedules of the 8th through 14th Censuses of the United States, 1860–1920: Virginia, Washington, D.C., and Massachusetts. U.S. Bureau of the Census, Washington, D.C.: National Archives and Records Administration. Database on-line. Provo, Utah: The Generations Network, Inc., 2005. http://www.ancestry.com/search/rectype/census/usfedcen/default.aspx.

U.S. Records of the General Accounting Office, Records of the Third Auditor's Office, Southern Claims Commission Case Files, 1871–1880. Virginia: Shenandoah to Spotsylvania Counties, Record Group 217, National Archives and Records Administration.

The War of the Rebellion: A Compilation of the Official Records of the Union and Confederate Armies. 256 vols. Washington, D.C.: U.S. War Department, 1880–1901.

WPA Description of Matthew Fountaine Maury Home.

Newspapers

Free Lance-Star (Fredericksburg, Va.). 4–22 May 1864.

New York Herald

Richmond Daily Dispatch. http://dlxs.richmond.edu/d/ddr/.

Virginia Herald

Theses and Dissertations

Bromberg, Alan Bruce. "Slavery in the Virginia Tobacco Factories, 1800–1860." M.A. thesis, University of Virginia, 1968.

Harcourt, Edward J. "The Civil War and Social Change: White Women in Fredericksburg, Virginia." Master's thesis. University of Richmond, 1997.

Sorensen, Leni. "Absconded: Fugitive Slaves in the Daybook of the Richmond Police Guard." Ph.D. dissertation, College of William and Mary, 2005.

Printed Sources

Abrahams, Roger D. *Singing the Master: The Emergence of African American Culture in the Plantation South.* New York: Pantheon, 1992.

Amann, William Frayne. *Personnel of the Civil War.* Vol. 2, *The Union Armies.* New York: Thomas Yoseloff, 1961.

Andrews, Ethan Allen. *Slavery and the Domestic Slave-Trade in the United States.* Boston: Light and Stearns, 1836.

Aptheker, Herbert. *Negro Slave Revolts in the United States, 1526–1860.* New York: International Publishers, 1939.

Ash, Stephen V. *Middle Tennessee Society Transformed, 1860–1870: War and Peace in the Upper South.* Baton Rouge: Louisiana State University Press, 1988.

Ayers, Edward L. *Vengeance and Justice: Crime and Punishment in the Nineteenth-Century American South.* New York: Oxford University Press, 1984.

Ayers, Edward L., Gary W. Gallagher, and Andrew J. Torget, eds. *Crucible of the Civil War: Virginia from Secession to Commemoration.* Charlottesville: University of Virginia Press, 2006.

Blackford, Launcelot Minor. *Mine Eyes Have Seen the Glory: The Story of a Virginia Lady, Mary Berkeley Minor Blackford, 1802–1896, Who Taught Her Sons to Hate Slavery and to Love the Union.* Cambridge, Mass.: Harvard University Press, 1954.

Blair, W. A. "Barbarians at Fredericksburg's Gate: The Impact of the Union Army on Civilians." In *The Fredericksburg Campaign: Decision on the Rappahannock,* edited by Gary W. Gallagher. Chapel Hill: University of North Carolina Press, 1995.

Blassingame, John W. *The Slave Community: Plantation Life in the Antebellum South.* New York: Oxford University Press, 1972.

———. *Black New Orleans, 1860–1880.* Chicago: University of Chicago Press, 1973.

Davis, Noah. *A Narrative of the Life of Rev. Noah Davis, a Colored Man, Written by Himself, at the Age of Fifty-Four.* Baltimore: John F. Weishampel, Jr., 1859.

D'Entremont, John. *Southern Emancipator: Moncure Conway, the American Years, 1832–1865.* New York: Oxford University Press, 1987.

Deyle, Steven. "The Domestic Slave Trade in America: The Lifeblood of the Southern Slave System." In *The Chattel Principle: Internal Slave Trades in the Americas,* edited by Walter Johnson. New Haven: Yale University Press, 2004. 91–116.

———. *Carry Me Back: The Domestic Slave Trade in American Life.* New York: Oxford University Press, 2005.

Dodd, Donald B., comp. *Historical Statistics of the States of the United States: Two Centuries of the Census, 1790–1990.* Westport, Conn.: Greenwood Press, 1993.

Douglass, Frederick. *Narrative of the Life of Frederick Douglass, an American Slave, Written by Himself.* Boston: Published at the Anti-Slavery Office, 1845. Electronic edition: http://docsouth.unc.edu/neh/douglass/douglass.html.

———. *My Bondage and My Freedom.* New York: Miller, Orton & Mulligan, 1855. Electronic edition: http://docsouth.unc.edu/neh/douglass55/douglass55.html.

Dove, Vee. *Madison County Homes: A Collection of Pre–Civil War Homes and Family Heritages.* Kingsport, Tenn.: Kingsport Press, 1975.

Druyvesteyn, K. "The James River and Kanawha Canal: A Pictorial Essay." *Virginia Cavalcade* 21, no. 3 (1972): 22–47.

Duff, John B., and Peter M. Mitchell, eds. *The Nat Turner Rebellion: The Historical Event and the Modern Controversy.* New York: Harper & Row, 1971.

Durrill, Wayne K. "Routine of Seasons: Labour Regimes and Social Ritual in an Antebellum Plantation Community." *Slavery and Abolition* 16, no. 2 (August 1995): 161–87.

Eicher, David J. *The Longest Night: A Military History of the Civil War.* New York: Simon & Schuster, 2001.

Elkins, Stanley M. *Slavery: A Problem in American Institutional and Intellectual Life.* 2nd ed. Chicago: University of Chicago Press, 1968.

Escott, Paul D. *Slavery Remembered: A Record of Twentieth-Century Slave Narratives.* Chapel Hill: University of North Carolina Press, 1979.

Fischer, David Hackett, and James C. Kelly. *Away, I'm Bound Away: Virginia and the Westward Movement.* Richmond: Virginia Historical Society, 1993.

Fisher, Therese A., comp. *Marriage Records of the City of Fredericksburg, and of Orange, Spotsylvania, and Stafford Counties, Virginia, 1722–1850.* 2nd ed. Bowie, Md.: Heritage Books, 1990.

Fitzgerald, Ruth Coder. *A Different Story: A Black History of Fredericksburg, Stafford, and Spotsylvania, Virginia.* Greensboro, N.C.: Unicorn, 1979.

Genovese, Eugene D. "The Treatment of Slaves in Different Countries: Problems in the Application of the Comparative Method." In *Slavery in the New World: A Reader in Comparative History,* edited by Laura Foner and Eugene D. Genovese, 202-10. Englewood Cliffs, N.J.: Prentice-Hall, 1969.

———. *Roll, Jordan, Roll: The World the Slaves Made.* New York: Pantheon, 1974.

———. *From Rebellion to Revolution: Afro-American Slave Revolts in the Making of the Modern World.* Baton Rouge: Louisiana State University Press, 1979.

Gerteis, Louis S. *From Contraband to Freedman: Federal Policy Toward Southern Blacks, 1861–1865.* Westport, Conn.: Greenwood Press, 1973.

Getz, Elizabeth. "'Take a Good Ready and Start Monday Morning': Abraham Lincoln in Fredericksburg, May 1862." *Journal of Fredericksburg History* 4 (1999): 16–35.

Goldfield, David R. *Urban Growth in the Age of Sectionalism: Virginia, 1847–1861.* Baton Rouge: Louisiana State University Press, 1977.

Goodheart, Lawrence B., Richard D. Brown, and Stephen G. Rabe, eds. *Slavery in American Society.* 3rd ed. Lexington, Mass.: D. C. Heath and Co., 1992.

Hall, Hillman Allyn. *History of the Sixth New York Cavalry (Second Ira Harris Guard) Second Brigade—First Division—Cavalry Corps, Army of the Potomac, 1861–1865.* Worcester, Mass.: Blanchard Press, 1908.

Harrison, Noel G. *Fredericksburg Civil War Sites.* 2 vols. Lynchburg, Va.: H. E. Howard, 1995. Vol. 1, *April 1861–November 1862.* Vol. 2, *December 1862–April 1865.*

Heidler, David S., and Jeanne T. Heidler, eds. *Encyclopedia of the American Civil*

War: A Political, Social, and Military History. 5 vols. Santa Barbara, Calif.: ABC-CLIO, 2000.

Herdegen, Lance J., and Sherry Murphy, eds. *Four Years with the Iron Brigade: The Civil War Journals of William R. Ray, Co. F., Seventh Wisconsin Infantry.* Cambridge, Mass.: Da Capo Press, 2002.

Hodge, Robert A., comp. *The Civil War Diary of Betty Herndon Maury (June 3, 1861–February 18, 1863).* Fredericksburg: Privately printed, 1985.

————. *Fredericksburg, Virginia, Death Records, 1853–1895.* Bowie, Md.: Heritage Books, 1991.

Isaac, Rhys. *The Transformation of Virginia, 1740–1790.* Chapel Hill: University of North Carolina Press, 1982.

Jackson, Luther Porter. *Free Negro Labor and Property Holding in Virginia, 1830–1860.* New York: D. Appleton-Century Co., 1942.

Johnson, Walter. *Soul by Soul: Life Inside the Antebellum Slave Market.* Cambridge, Mass.: Harvard University Press, 1999.

The Journal of Jane Howison Beale of Fredericksburg, Virginia, 1850–1862. Fredericksburg, Va.: Historic Fredericksburg, 1979.

Klingberg, Frank Wysor. *The Southern Claims Commission.* Millwood, N.Y.: Kraus Reprint, 1980.

Krick, Robert K. *30th Virginia Infantry.* Lynchburg, Va.: H. E. Howard, 1983.

Levine, Lawrence W. *Black Culture and Black Consciousness: Afro-American Folk Thought from Slavery to Freedom.* New York: Oxford University Press, 1977.

McPherson, James M., ed. *Encyclopedia of Civil War Biographies.* Vol. 1. Armonk, N.Y.: Sharpe Reference, 2000.

Mackay, Alexander. *The Western World; or, Travels in the United States in 1846–47: Exhibiting Them in Their Latest Development, Social, Political and Industrial, Including a Chapter on California.* Vol. I. Philadelphia: Lea & Blanchard, 1849.

Mitchell, Reid. *The Vacant Chair: The Northern Soldier Leaves Home.* New York: Oxford University Press, 1993.

Olmsted, Frederick Law. *A Journey in the Seaboard Slave States, with Remarks on their Economy.* New York: Dix and Edwards, 1856.

Painter, Nell Irvin. "Representing Truth: Sojourner Truth's Knowing and Becoming Known." *Journal of American History* 81, no. 2 (1994): 461–92.

Parish, Peter J. *Slavery: History and Historians.* New York: Harper & Row, 1989.

Patrick, Marsena Rudolph. *Inside Lincoln's Army: The Diary of Marsena Rudolph Patrick, Provost Marshall General, Army of the Potomac.* Edited by David S. Sparks. New York: Thomas Yoseloff, 1964.

Patterson, Orlando. *Slavery and Social Death: A Comparative Study.* Cambridge, Mass.: Harvard University Press, 1982.

Perdue, Charles L., Jr., Thomas E. Barden, and Robert K. Phillips, eds. *Weevils in the Wheat: Interviews with Virginia Ex-Slaves.* Charlottesville: University Press of Virginia, 1976.

Phillips, Ulrich B. *American Negro Slavery: A Survey of the Supply, Employment, and Control of Negro Labor as Determined by the Plantation Regime.* Baton Rouge: Louisiana State University Press, 1966.

Quenzel, Carrol H. *The History and Background of St. George's Episcopal Church, Fredericksburg, Virginia.* Richmond: Privately printed, 1951.

Quinn, S. J. *The History of the City of Fredericksburg, Virginia.* Richmond: Heritage Press, 1908.

Rable, George C. *Fredericksburg! Fredericksburg!* Chapel Hill: University of North Carolina Press, 2002.

Raboteau, Albert J. *Slave Religion: The "Invisible Institution" in the Antebellum South.* New York: Oxford University Press, 1978.

Ramage, James A. *Gray Ghost: The Life of Col. John Singleton Mosby.* Lexington: University Press of Kentucky, 1999.

Rose, Willie Lee. *A Documentary History of Slavery in North America.* New York: Oxford University Press, 1976.

Rothman, David J. *The Discovery of the Asylum: Social Order and Disorder in the New Republic.* Boston: Little, Brown, 1971.

Russell, Robert. *North America, Its Agriculture and Climate: Containing Observations on the Agriculture and Climate of Canada, the United States, and the Island of Cuba.* Edinburgh: Adam and Charles Black, 1857.

Salmon, Emily J., and Edward D. C. Campbell, Jr., eds. *The Hornbook of Virginia History: A Ready-Reference Guide to the Old Dominion's People, Places, and Past.* 4th ed. Richmond: Library of Virginia, 1994.

Sifakis, Stewart. *Who Was Who in the Civil War.* New York: Facts on File, 1988.

Stuckey, Sterling. *Slave Culture: Nationalist Theory and the Foundations of Black America.* New York: Oxford University Press, 1987.

Sutherland, Daniel E. *Seasons of War: The Ordeal of a Confederate Community, 1861–1865.* New York: Free Press, 1995.

Tadman, Michael. *Speculators and Slaves: Masters, Traders, and Slaves in the Old South.* Madison: University of Wisconsin Press, 1989.

Thornton, John. *Africa and Africans in the Making of the Atlantic World, 1400–1680.* Cambridge: Cambridge University Press, 1992.

Turner, Charles W. "The Early Railroad Movement in Virginia." *Virginia Magazine of History and Biography* 55 (1947): 350–71.

———. "Railroad Service to Virginia Farmers, 1828–1860." *Agricultural History* 22 (1948): 239–47.

Wade, Richard C. *Slavery in the Cities: The South, 1820–1860.* New York: Oxford University Press, 1964.

Warner, Ezra J. *Generals in Blue: Lives of the Union Commanders.* Baton Rouge: Louisiana State University Press, 1964.

Workers of the Writers' Program of the Work Projects Administration in the State of Virginia, comp. *Virginia: A Guide to the Old Dominion.* Richmond: Virginia State Library and Archives, 1992.

————. *The Negro in Virginia.* Winston-Salem: John F. Blair, 1994.

Wyatt-Brown, Bertram. *Southern Honor: Ethics and Behavior in the Old South.* New York: Oxford University Press, 1982.

INDEX

Washington, Booker T., xxx, 5
Washington, Charles (son), 79
Washington, George, 24, 58
Washington, James (cousin), 47
Washington, James (son), 79
Washington, John: assigned to Gen. King,
50; baptism, 31; birth, 1; and breaking
up of slave families, xxiii–xxv, 11, 13,
16, 30–31; childhood memories, 1–3;
6–7; children of, 79; and Christmas
rations, xiv, 3, 9–10; compared to
Frederick Douglass, xi–xiii; and Confederate efforts to frighten slaves, 43–44;
conversion, 28; courting, 28, 31; dissimulation, 12, 20–21, 25, 39, 46; and
fairs, xiv, 10, 27–28; family after Civil
War, 79; family members, 11, 16; first
night of freedom, 49; "Godmother" of,
2; grandmother and aunt mentioned,
6, 68, 78; hiring out, xi, xii, 5, 29, 33,
36, 38–39, 42; and hog killing, 3, 8–9;
identity of father, 4; importance of
mother, xxxi, 1–2, 4, 7, 11, 16, 22, 27;
30; joins Union forces, 47–48; keeps a
diary, 1, 4–5; last Fredericksburg visit,
76; learning to read and write, xxxi,
11–12, 17–18, 20, 29, 36; and master-
slave relations, 7–8; and meaning of
freedom, xiv–xv, xxviii–xxix, xxxi, 5,
8, 10, 14, 17, 25–27, 30–31, 33, 45,
49, 65, 74–75, 81; and slave treatment,
7–8; tobacco factory work, 30; and
train accident, 22; and typhoid fever,
29; uncle in Detroit, 39; understanding
of Civil War, xiv–xv; understanding
of literacy, xxx, xxxi, 12, 17; and
Union troops' funeral, 49–50; in
Warrenton, 67
Washington, John (son), 79
Washington, William (son), 79
Weedon, George, 24
Whites, ideals of, xiv
Willis Mills, 1, 6
Wood, Charles, 50, 61; takes prisoners in
Fredericksburg, 51, 55
Woolfolk, Sally, 91
Wynne, Elizabeth Maxwell, 78

Zook, Samuel K. (Fifty-seventh New York
Infantry), 59